Encountering Jesus at Chr

Cultivating a heart of expectanc

But Mary treasured up all these things, po

As we approach Christmas together, life becomes busier with socialising, shopping, and celebrating. All too easily we run out of time to be still and ponder, just like Jesus' mother, Mary (Luke 2:19). These devotionals are the product of prayer aimed to give each of us a few moments to contemplate God, the reason for Christmas, our chance to listen carefully and discover what God is saying to us this Christmas.

I'm also thrilled that after writing EDWJ for the last two years I can introduce a fresh author for this edition. Keith Foster served in the Royal Navy before moving into industry, where he heard, pondered, and then responded to God's call to the work of an evangelist and church pastor. He has a wealth of experience in loving and serving God, as well as enabling others to find and deepen their faith. Last year he joined our Waverley Abbey team to create and lead our successful Contemporary Chaplaincy course, and now serves as Head of Waverley's Vocational Courses. We've just launched Contemporary Discipleship and Contemporary Church Ministry alongside Chaplaincy. He has completed his doctoral studies looking at sharing the Christian faith with those who find themselves at the edge of society, as reflected in Jesus' ministry throughout Luke's Gospel.

Christmas, whilst familiar, is a wonderful time to contemplate the sacrificial love of God. Jesus stepped away from the familiarity of heaven, the intimate relationship with His Father and the Spirit, to live as man and God bringing the eternal message of salvation, the recovery of humanity's lost friendship with God. Use these weeks to consider your friendship with God? If there's a need for some restoration work, then take the opportunity to surrender to God afresh. If you've never encountered God, then this Christmas ask for God's forgiveness and place your life in His hands. If you make that prayer your own then email me your address so I can send you a complimentary copy of, *Every Day with Jesus for New Christians*.

Thanks for joining us as we approach Christmas. If you have any feedback, questions, or prayer requests please email me, micha@edwj.org.

Every blessing, Dr Micha Jazz – Head of Waverley Abbey Ministries

At a **Glance**

Is God calling you to mentorship or coaching?

The Christian context for mentorship and coaching centres around coming alongside someone in their spiritual growth. That may be an overt objective, if your mentee is committed to discipleship. Or it may be more subtle spiritual support, like helping a prison leaver restore their life in a healthy way.

What's important in a mentor is a willing heart to invest in another person's life. You care about their goals, and their path to achieving their potential, and becoming more like Jesus. You're helping that person realise who God created them to be and discovering the unique gifts they have to offer the world.

Does that thought light you up?

Maybe God is calling you to take on that role in someone's life. You could be the right person to mentor (i) a university student, (ii) a person who is recently engaged or newlywed (iii) a person leaving prison, or (iv) a member of your congregation. Ask the Holy Spirit to bring someone to mind if you're not sure.

While a coaching or mentoring relationship is about investing in somebody else, you may be surprised by what God teaches you through the process. Like it says in Proverbs, "as iron sharpens iron, so one person sharpens another" (27:17). You may find new avenues in your journey with God as you come alongside another person.

If God's calling you towards mentoring or coaching, we can equip you with the knowledge and the tools you need to take on the role responsibly. You'll have not only the qualifications, but also the community around you that can cover you in prayer, and provide you with practical tips and spiritual support when you need it.

To sign up for a certificate in mentoring and coaching, taught in Farnham, please visit our website: **waverleyabbeycollege.ac.uk**

Every day with Jesus - Spring Harvest Holidays

Join us on our second Every Day with Jesus holiday retreat. Micha and Jayne Jazz invite you to Spring Harvest Holidays in Le Pas Opton, France from May 22-26 (departure May 27) for five days of relaxation, refreshment, and spiritual renewal.

Le Pas Opton offers a high quality and chilled holiday environment for personal and family rest and refuelling; physically, mentally, and spiritually. Here Micha and Jayne will lead a brief time of worship and bible engagement each morning to focus our hearts on encountering God on our holiday. Each evening there will be

the opportunity to close our day with Compline and Examen at 9.30 pm, with conversation and drinks in the bar to follow. The rest of the day is for fun and adventure, including shared activities for any who want to holiday together, whilst deepening their faith. Here friendships are forged and faith deepened.

Please visit **springharvestholidays.com/retreat** or email **micha@edwj.org** for more information.

This will prove a time of rest with the opportunity for a fresh encounter with God, so we can return with greater confidence in how we can practically live every day with Jesus.

A chat **with...**

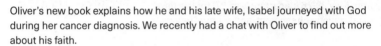

Oliver Vellacott

Author of *Living with Cancer, Walking with God*

Oliver's new book explains how he and his late wife, Isabel journeyed with God during her cancer diagnosis. We recently had a chat with Oliver to find out more about his faith.

What are the ways in which you spend every day with Jesus?
Do you mind if I turn this around and say this; Jesus spends every day with me. He has, after all, promised never to leave me and He doesn't change (Hebrews 13:5-8). In my late teens I had a vision of Jesus which was overwhelming, and that encounter endures to this day, albeit not in such a visual way.

What practices do you find helpful to align your heart and mind with Jesus?
I set aside time each morning to read Scripture. I write my own responses to the passage and then write my 'journal' detailing experiences of the previous day. In the evening I enjoy daily readings in the Psalms with Tim Keller's book *My Rock, my Refuge.*

Do you have any tips for reading the Bible / engaging with Scripture?
I am often amazed during Bible study by the things others glean from a passage that I have missed. God does speak to us individually from His Word. My advice would be; don't feel you have to be prescriptive in Bible study but instead ask, "What is God saying to me today?"

Do you prepare yourself spiritually for Christmas in any particular way?
In recent years I have enjoyed reading Sinclair Ferguson's *Daily meditations for Advent.*

Thanks Oliver. If you want to find out more about Oliver's walk with God and how he and Isabel handled her cancer journey, you can get *Living with Cancer, Walking with God*, from **wvly.org/lwc**

Living with Cancer
&
Walking with God

Isabel and Oliver Vellacott

Encountering Jesus at Christmas time

Our purpose in *Every Day with Jesus* is to learn how we interact with Jesus, and how Jesus interacts with us. Encounters with Jesus deepen our faith and create intimacy with our Creator. We're all looking for more encounters, aren't we?

Of course, Jesus doesn't wait until Christmas to pursue relationship with us. But it is a special time of year, when we think more intentionally about Jesus' arrival on Earth. So Christmas time presents an opportunity to encounter Jesus in a different way to the rest of the year.

There's a tradition of signs and wonders at this time of year. We all know the nativity story, with the magi following a bright star, and shepherds being drawn to the stable. What signs and wonders is God sending to you this year? It may be a robin who pops up every morning in your garden. Or a chance sighting of a shooting star. Perhaps it's an unexpected gift. God is always speaking, so keep your ears and eyes peeled for signs and wonders as evidence of encounters with Jesus.

Hospitality is a key feature of this season. Jesus loves to join your party! Are your senses attuned to Jesus' presence during dinner? You might feel a sense of that 'at home' peacefulness. Or a wry feeling that somebody is smiling with content at this gathering of friends and family.

Some encounters are subtle. As Tim Keller says: "God has given us many gifts – vulnerability for intimacy, comfort for suffering, passion for justice, and power over prejudice" Perhaps your encounter with Jesus is unexpected vulnerability with a loved one. Or moments of relief from long-experienced suffering.

We'd love to hear about your encounters with Jesus this season. Please share your experiences on the Facebook group, or simply email Micha at **micha@edwj.org**

Matthew 3:13–17
'And a voice from heaven said, "This is my Son, whom I love; with him I am well pleased."' (v17)

'How can Jesus love me?' This is something we hear frequently from all sorts of people living with guilt, regret and shame – perhaps those who think they are beyond God's love, or those who keep stumbling over the same habitual issues. Yet, in order to understand the depth of Christ's love for us, it is helpful to primarily think about the love that exists within the Trinity. We see this in the baptism of Jesus, where in Matthew chapter 3, verses 16–17 we read: 'As soon as Jesus was baptised, he went up out of the water. At that moment heaven was opened, and he saw the Spirit of God descending like a dove and alighting on him. And a voice from heaven said, "This is my Son, *whom I love*; with him I am well pleased' (italics mine).

The love expressed by God the Father, towards His Son, witnessed by the Spirit, is *unquestionable* – yet how does this encourage us? With that unquestionable love in mind, Jesus tells us in John 15, verse 9: 'As the Father has loved me, so have I loved you.' The *same* love that exists between the Trinity, is the love that is lavished upon us. God's love towards you is unquestionable, and it is in this we can rest. As the hymnwriter puts it:

Oh love that will not let me go
I rest my weary soul in you
I give you back the life I owe
That in your ocean depths its flow
May richer, fuller be.*

SCRIPTURE TO CONSIDER: Jer. 31:3; John 15:9–17; 1 John 4:19

AN ACTION TO TAKE: Think about the extent of the love between Father, Son and Holy Spirit, and then ponder Jesus' words: 'As the Father has loved me, so have I loved you.' Offer up praise and thanks for His unquestionable love.

A PRAYER TO MAKE: 'Lord, thank You that Your love for me is unquestionable. Amen.'

*George Matheson, 1842–1906

John 13:31–38
'A new command I give you: love one another. As I have loved you, so you must love one another. By this everyone will know that you are my disciples, if you love one another.' (vv34–35)

As children of God, knowing we are loved by Him makes all the difference in our day-to-day lives, service and walk with Him. A loved child is a secure child. Yet God's love is not something we are to simply cling onto for our own benefit, but rather is something to 'pass on'.

Within our scripture reading today, having just washed the disciples' feet, modelling what true love and service looks like, Jesus then says to the disciples, 'A new command I give you: love one another. As I have loved you, so you must love one another' (v34).

Whenever we are commanded to do something in Scripture, it is because we do not naturally do it – in other words, we don't have to be commanded to do things we naturally do. Yet the command to love each other was not new, the disciples knew from the law and the prophets that they were to love their neighbour (Lev. 19:18). However, Jesus, soon to demonstrate His supreme act of love at the cross, points His disciples to a new, purer, deeper, divine level of love: 'love one another. As I have loved you' (v34a).

The unquestionable, unconditional love Jesus has lavished on us (John 15:9), is to be 'passed on' to one another. The result? 'Everyone will know that you are my disciples.'

SCRIPTURE TO CONSIDER: Lev. 19:1–18; Deut. 10:12–22; Rom. 13:8–10; Gal. 5:13–26

AN ACTION TO TAKE: Think about the love of God for you. How might you be able to 'pass this on' today?

A PRAYER TO MAKE: 'Lord, thank You that You first loved us, and demonstrated what true love is, that we might love others too. Amen.'

John 15:9–17
**'My command is this: love each other as I have
loved you. Greater love has no one than this: to lay
down one's life for one's friends.' (vv12–13)**

Knowing we are loved and being commanded to love others is one
thing, but knowing what that truly looks like is another. There are
many ways love can be demonstrated, in word and deed: both are
important – in fact essential – if our lives are to be authentic reflections
of the God who first loved us (1 John 4:19). Yet in our scripture reading
today, Jesus points to the supreme act of love He was about to
demonstrate when He said to His disciples, 'Greater love has no one
than this: to lay down one's life for one's friends' (v13).

Referring to His imminent, selfless, loving act on the cross, Jesus
would go on to demonstrate what true, unconditional, sacrificial love
looked like, by offering Himself as a sacrifice for our sin. Romans
chapter 3, verse 25 tells us, 'God presented Christ as a sacrifice of
atonement, through the shedding of his blood – to be received by faith.'
Sacrificial love always has the 'other' in mind; the greater good, the
bigger picture. As loved Christ-followers today, if we need an example
of what sacrificial love truly looks like, we need look no farther than the
cross. The chorus says:

Such love, pure as the whitest snow,
Such love, weeps for the shame I know,
Such love, paying the debt I owe,
O Jesus, such love.*

SCRIPTURE TO CONSIDER: Ps. 13:1–6 & 33:1–22; Rom. 3:21–26; Heb. 7:11–28

AN ACTION TO TAKE: Think about the sacrificial love of Christ for you. How might
we give ourselves to others to model this love?

A PRAYER TO MAKE: 'Lord, thank You for the cross, for showing us what true
sacrificial love looks like. Amen.'

*Graham Kendrick, Make Way Music, 1988.

2 Corinthians 5:16–21

'God made him who had no sin to be sin for us, so that in him we might become the righteousness of God.' (v21)

The meaning of words can change over time. What something meant in one generation, may not always be obvious in another. Today, when we think of the word 'substitute', our immediate thoughts may turn to sport, where a like-for-like replacement is tactically brought in to play as the team manager seeks victory. However, in the Bible, substitute is one metaphor that is given to speak of Christ's atoning work on the cross for us. Verse 21 of 2 Corinthians 5 tells us, 'God made Him who had no sin to be sin for us, so that in him we might become the righteousness of God.' In our hopeless state, staring sin and death in the face, the perfect, sinless Son of God, Jesus, became our substitute, and in our place died on the cross, defeating sin. Yet it did not stop there: three days later Jesus was raised to life, defeating death itself, snatching victory out of defeat (1 Cor. 15:3–4). The apostle Paul, in unfettered celebration of this, could write, 'Where, O death, is your victory? Where, O death, is your sting? The sting of death is sin, and the power of sin is the law. But thanks be to God! He gives us the victory through our Lord Jesus Christ' (1 Cor. 15:55–57). As those who have trusted Christ, who lean on and put our hope in the finished work of our glorious substitute, Jesus, we too can celebrate and sing the words of the hymn:

> Bearing shame and scoffing rude,
> In my place condemned He stood,
> Sealed my pardon with His blood,
> Hallelujah, what a Saviour!*

SCRIPTURE TO CONSIDER: Gen. 22:1–19; Isa. 53:1–12; 1 Cor. 15:1–58; Heb. 9:1–14

AN ACTION TO TAKE: Think about the spaces and places we find ourselves in every day. How might we point people to the One who has defeated sin and death?

A PRAYER TO MAKE: 'Lord, thank You for taking my place, for taking the punishment that my sin and rebellion deserved. Help me to serve You with unfettered joy. Amen.'

*P.P. Bliss, 1875.

Romans 12:1–21

'Therefore, I urge you, brothers and sisters, in view of God's mercy, to offer your bodies as a living sacrifice, holy and pleasing to God – this is your true and proper worship. Do not conform to the pattern of this world, but be transformed by the renewing of your mind. Then you will be able to test and approve what God's will is – his good, pleasing and perfect will.' (vv1–2)

Sacrifice in the Bible involved death. In the Old Testament, various animals were sacrificed (e.g. Gen. 8:20; Exod. 29:36). In the New Testament, it is Jesus, the spotless lamb of God, whose blood is shed (Heb. 9:12). As we consider the sacrifice of Christ, the One who became sin for us (2 Cor. 5:21), there is only one fitting response, and that is to give ourselves wholeheartedly to Him. Yet, in what seems like a paradox, the apostle Paul in verse 1 of Romans 12, calls us to be *living* sacrifices. How can this be?

As living sacrifices, death does indeed take place, a dying to our old selves. To the Galatian church Paul could say, 'I have been crucified with Christ and I no longer live, but Christ lives in me. The life I now live in the body, I live by faith in the Son of God, who loved me and gave himself for me' (Gal. 2:20). Sacrificial living means dying to self. As C.T. Studd, the founder of the WEC mission organisation said, 'If Jesus Christ be God and died for me, then no sacrifice can be too great for me to make for Him.'

As we seek to live for Him - may we offer our time, talent and treasure to Him - asking Him to use it for His glory.

SCRIPTURE TO CONSIDER: Ps. 1:1–6; Neh. 13:1–31; 1 Pet. 4:1–6; Phil. 3:1–14

AN ACTION TO TAKE: Think about anything in your life that detracts you from serving the Lord wholeheartedly. Offer this up to God.

A PRAYER TO MAKE: 'Lord, help me to be a living sacrifice for You. By Your Spirit, help me to eradicate those things in me which dishonour and misrepresent You. Amen.'

Heartfelt Service

Psalm 51:1–19

'You do not delight in sacrifice, or I would bring it; you do not take pleasure in burnt offerings. My sacrifice, O God, is a broken spirit; a broken and contrite heart you, God, will not despise.' (vv16–17)

Sacrificially serving the Lord is one thing, but this in itself can become unhealthy if done with impure motives or as a means to demonstrate our spirituality. King David, after committing adultery and murder (2 Sam. 11), thought he could carry on in His God-appointed role without being held accountable. However, verse 27 of 2 Samuel 11 tells us that, 'the thing David had done displeased the LORD'. This led to the Lord admonishing David through the prophet Nathan (2 Sam. 12:1–12). Convicted by the Lord's words, David subsequently confessed, 'I have sinned against the LORD' (2 Sam. 12:13). Having further reflected on his actions, David penned Psalm 51, where he would write, 'My sacrifice, O God, is a broken spirit; a broken and contrite heart you, God, will not despise' (v17).

Religious service and sacrifice are no substitute for service that arises out of brokenness and thankfulness. The apostle Paul, in 1 Corinthians chapter 1, verses 26–31, tells us that, 'God chose the lowly things of this world... so that no-one may boast.' As we realise our weakness and brokenness before a holy God, and as we offer ourselves to Him with a contrite spirit, in true, heartfelt service, this is true worship.

It is only in the light of His holiness when compared to our brokenness and imperfections - that our service becomes authentic and Christ-centred as we offer our broken selves to Him.

SCRIPTURE TO CONSIDER: Isa. 57:14–21 & 66:1–22; 1 Cor. 1:18–31; 2 Cor. 12:1–10

AN ACTION TO TAKE: Think about your motivation for service. Is there anything in your life that you need to take time to confess?

A PRAYER TO MAKE: 'Lord, I pray that my busyness will not be a barrier to hearing Your voice, to receiving Your correction. Create in me a clean heart, O God, and renew a right spirit within me. Amen.'

John 21:1–25

'The third time he said to him, "Simon son of John, do you love me?" Peter was hurt because Jesus asked him the third time, "Do you love me?" He said, "Lord, you know all things; you know that I love you." Jesus said, "Feed my sheep."' (v17)

It can be easy when thinking of the various Bible characters, to think of them as perfect exemplars of service to God. Yet a detailed study of their lives, as depicted in the Bible, gives us a different picture. Abraham lied about Sarah being his sister (Gen. 20:2). King David committed adultery and murder (2 Sam. 11). John Mark deserted the apostle Paul on his first mission trip (Acts 13:13). Peter denied having ever known the Lord (Mark 14:66–72). Thinking about Peter, after denying that he ever knew Jesus, Peter went back to his old life, to what he knew, to being a fisherman. Perhaps Peter thought his days of being used by God were over. Maybe the earlier promises of Jesus in Matthew 16, verse 18, that Peter would be a key figure in the building of Christ's Church, were null and void.

Yet letting God down and misrepresenting His character in some way, does not have to be permanent or fatal. In John chapter 21, we see the resurrected Jesus, reinstate Peter, re-affirming him in his calling to shepherd God's people – to go on with God. Perhaps we feel we have let God down, disqualifying us from service. Whilst it is important to maturely reflect on our failures and shortcomings, they can helpfully shape us, but should never define us. We need to allow the Lord's Word and calling to come to us afresh, to reinstate us, and to encourage us to get on with the task He has called us to do.

SCRIPTURE TO CONSIDER: Jer. 15:1–21; Hos. 14:1–9; Luke 17:1–10; 1 John 1:1–10

AN ACTION TO TAKE: Are we paralysed by our past failures – struggling to move on in loving service to the Lord? Receive His commission, allowing His Spirit to re-instate us, using the gifts He has given us.

A PRAYER TO MAKE: 'Lord, thank You that I am not the sum of my past failures and that Your Word of re-instatement comes to commission me. Help me to receive it with a thankful heart. Amen.'

Philippians 3:1–14

'But whatever were gains to me I now consider loss for the sake of Christ. What is more, I consider everything a loss because of the surpassing worth of knowing Christ Jesus my Lord, for whose sake I have lost all things.' (vv7–8)

Knowing what matters is an essential quality in life and work. If we react to everything in the same way, or treat everything with the same priority, then we risk focusing on the wrong things, or allowing less important matters to distract us from those that really matter. The apostle Paul knew what really mattered. Reflecting back on his 'old way of life', where as a Pharisee he would have been recognised and revered, the apostle tells us that this paled into insignificance in comparison to knowing and following Jesus, 'for whose sake [he had] lost all things' (v8b).

It can be easy for us today to be distracted from our pursuit of knowing and following Christ. Long working hours, paying the bills, family, friends – all important, yet all needing to be kept in balance as we seek to serve King Jesus. There may also be other things that we need to jettison: unhelpful distractions, habits, even influences. As we focus on knowing and following Christ, perspective can be gained on everything else, as Jesus said, 'Seek first his kingdom and his righteousness, and all these things will be given to you as well' (Matt. 6:33).

Maybe it is time for each of us to ask ourselves what really matters - giving all we do to Him and for His Kingdom service.

SCRIPTURE TO CONSIDER: Ps. 112:1–10; Isa. 26:1–21; Matt. 6:25–34; Heb. 12:1–3

AN ACTION TO TAKE: Think about those things that take our time and that we prioritise. Do they help or hinder our focus on Christ?

A PRAYER TO MAKE: 'Lord, help me to know what really matters, to focus on Your things, Your calling and plans for my life, Your kingdom. Amen.'

Doing it for God

Colossians 3:1–25
'And whatever you do, whether in word or deed, do it all in the name of the Lord Jesus, giving thanks to God the Father through him.' (v17)

It can be easy to compartmentalise our lives into the 'sacred' and the 'secular'. Perhaps the things we do 'in church' or that have an obvious link to faith, we consider to be more spiritual or sacred, with everything else considered to be a distraction from God's work – perhaps our job or family commitments. Such thinking can cause resentments, bitterness and arguments, perhaps thinking these 'secular' things are drawing us away from serving God.

This sort of thinking is a legacy of Greek influence on the early Church that tended to separate the material and the spiritual world, as opposed to a Hebraic mindset that sought to see God at work in the everyday. Likewise today, our mindset is strongly influenced by the culture we grew up and now live in – fish rarely question the water they swim in!

Yet to the Colossian church, Paul's exhortation is for them to consider everything they do as 'sacred', stating, 'whatever you do, whether in word or deed, do it all in the name of the Lord Jesus' (v17a). Paul then goes on in chapter three of Colossians to apply this broadly to the household and the workplace (vv18–25), encouraging them in 'whatever [they] do, [to] work at it with all [their] heart, as working for the Lord' (v23). Such an approach makes everything we do an act of worship and service to God. So, whether we are caring for children or other family members or friends, or working in the office, factory or community, we can do so knowing we are 'doing it for God'.

SCRIPTURE TO CONSIDER: Gen. 39:1–6a; Deut. 10:12–22; Eph. 6:1–9; Mark 9:30–37

AN ACTION TO TAKE: Offer each activity and task of the day to God as an act of worship and service.

A PRAYER TO MAKE: 'Lord, I give You back this day that You have given me. Whatever I do, I give it to You in complete service. Amen.'

Hebrews 10:19–25

'Let us hold unswervingly to the hope we profess, for he who promised is faithful. And let us consider how we may spur one another on towards love and good deeds, not giving up meeting together, as some are in the habit of doing, but encouraging one another – and all the more as you see the Day approaching.' (vv23–25)

As we serve the Lord each day, it is good to know we are part of the bigger, worldwide family of God. Yet, as with any family, at times, the various members can face trials and discouragements. Whilst some people may be happily serving and feeling blessed, others might be feeling isolated and discouraged. The Hebrews writer gives us an antidote to discouragement, by exhorting us to get involved with 'one another'. This includes spurring one another on (v24), encouraging each other to keep going. Essentially, this also involves regularly meeting together (v25a).

The recent pandemic made meeting together particularly challenging, and for many was cruel and isolating. Yet we can praise God that there are various ways of meeting, be that online or face to face. We can even encourage one another through letters and other written communication. Whichever method we choose, the important thing is that we 'one another' one another. Our motivation for doing so is two-fold. Firstly, we can encourage each other to 'hold unswervingly to the hope we profess' (v23). Secondly, we do so in the light of the Lord's return as we 'see the Day approaching' (v25). Keeping the wider family of God in mind, along with the encouragement of the Lord's return, can motivate us all to keep going.

SCRIPTURE TO CONSIDER: Prov. 27:17; John 13:31–34; Acts 2:42–47; Rom. 12:9–21

AN ACTION TO TAKE: How might you encourage someone today? Perhaps a call, a note or a visit.

A PRAYER TO MAKE: 'Lord, thank You for Your worldwide family. Help me to encourage my brothers and sisters, all the more as I see the Day approaching. Amen.'

Acts 2:42–47

'They devoted themselves to the apostles' teaching and to fellowship, to the breaking of bread and to prayer.' (v42)

Meeting together is one thing, but what should this look like? The question has been the cause of much discussion in churches throughout Church history. Debates about the décor, the time we meet, and other things, can cause unnecessary heartache and division. The Bible, perhaps frustratingly for some, gives us very little detail about 'how' and 'when' we meet. However, in Acts chapter 2, Luke gives us an insight into several characteristics of the Early Church gatherings. In verse 42 of chapter 2, we see that gathering to hear and discuss Scripture was important, as was meeting with other believers for fellowship. Remembering who they were gathered around was also central, as they broke bread together. Finally, Luke tells us that these early meetings were also characterised by prayer. The result of this focus was a church that regularly felt and saw the awesome activity of God (v43), sensed a unity (v44), and regularly helped each other with practical needs (v45). Ultimately, this thriving church grew as 'the Lord added to their number daily those who were being saved' (v47).

As we meet together, whatever the location, whatever time of day it may be, perhaps we too can focus on Scripture, sharing encouraging stories of God's working, with meetings centred around the life, death, resurrection and return of Jesus, characterised by prayer – and as we do so, let us also expect to see awesome acts of God, developing a wonderful unity, where each other's practical and spiritual needs are met, and growth is experienced.

SCRIPTURE TO CONSIDER: Neh. 8:1–18; Isa. 58:1–14; Acts 14:21–28; Rev. 3:7–22

AN ACTION TO TAKE: What contribution do we make to our gatherings? Do we seek to build up and encourage? Think about how you might do this within the context the Lord has placed you.

A PRAYER TO MAKE: 'Lord, thank You that as we gather, You are with us. Help us as we meet to focus on what matters. Amen.'

Psalm 1:1–6

'Blessed is the one... whose delight is in the law of the LORD, and who meditates on his law day and night. That person is like a tree planted by streams of water, which yields its fruit in season and whose leaf does not wither – whatever they do prospers.' (vv1–3)

The Bible is full of references to the benefits of allowing God's Word, the Bible, to inform, guide and direct our lives (Ps. 12:6 and 119:1–176). Another psalm, the very first psalm, gives us a picture of the life of someone whose 'delight is in the law of the LORD' (v2), describing such a person as, 'like a tree planted by streams of water, which yields its fruit in season' (v3a). This picture of a flourishing tree is used in other places within the Bible to depict spiritual flourishing (e.g. Jer. 17:7–9).

It can be easy in our busy world to allow ourselves to 'soak up' all sorts of information, some helpful, other sources not so. Yet a great habit to cultivate is the one of 'soaking' in God's Word. As we do so, we can expect a spiritually fruitful life. Additionally, when we face times of challenge, we can be confident that as those 'planted' in His Word, we will not wither under the heat of circumstance.

Alternatively, if we restrict our access to God's life-changing Word to the Sunday sermon, or occasional devotionals, it may not be surprising to find ourselves floundering in life's storms.

It is only as we are planted in His Word - empowered by His Spirit, that we become fruitful.

SCRIPTURE TO CONSIDER: Ps. 33 & 119; Jer. 17:5–18; Matt. 7:15–20

AN ACTION TO TAKE: How are we regularly planting ourselves in God's Word? Perhaps consider something from Waverley Abbey Resources to help you – our *Cover to Cover* series, for example.

A PRAYER TO MAKE: 'Lord, thank You for Your Word that nourishes us and helps us to flourish. Amen.'

Praising Him in Everything

Psalm 150:1–6
'Let everything that has breath praise the LORD.' (v6)

It can be difficult sometimes to feel like praising God, particularly if life's circumstances are challenging, with prolonged seasons of suffering or unanswered prayer. It is much easier to give thanks when things are going well, when we feel at ease and in a good place generally.

To the Thessalonian church, the apostle Paul could say, 'give thanks in all circumstances, for this is God's will for you in Christ Jesus' (1 Thess. 5:18). This was particularly difficult for the believers in Thessalonica who were under great persecution and who had lost dear brothers and sisters. Yet in our reading today, the psalmist exhorts everyone to 'praise the Lord', indeed the whole psalm is sandwiched by this exhortation in verses 1 and 6. This truly is a 'praise sandwich'!

The psalmist gives us several reasons to praise God. We are encouraged to praise Him for the ways in which we have seen Him powerfully work before (v2a). Additionally, we are called to praise Him simply for the fact that He alone is 'great' (v2b). Indeed, even as we have breath in our body, we are called to praise Him (v6). As long as the Lord gives us each breath, we can use it to praise Him with all we have. 'Let everything that has breath praise the Lord.'

Even if life is tough, facing challenge after challenge at the moment, every breath is a gift, giving the hope of a new day that has never been lived before - an opportunity to live for Him.

SCRIPTURE TO CONSIDER: Ps. 9:1–20 & 100:1–5; 1 Thess. 5:12–28; Jas 1:1–18

AN ACTION TO TAKE: Whatever our circumstances, we can give thanks to God – even for the breath in our body. Make a list of things you can give thanks for today.

A PRAYER TO MAKE: 'Lord, thank You that You see our challenges and difficulties, yet call us to give thanks to You in the midst of them. Thank You that it is in You that we "live and move and have our being". Amen.'

Matthew 28:16–20
'Therefore go and make disciples of all nations, baptising them in the name of the Father and of the Son and of the Holy Spirit, and teaching them to obey everything I have commanded you. And surely I am with you always, to the very end of the age.' (vv19–20)

When we face life's challenges, knowing that the Lord is with us is a supreme comfort. This can be more so as we face new chapters of uncertainty, perhaps a new job, moving home, a new calling or ministry. As we consider the Scriptures, we see the Lord encouraging His people to step into His purposes – to take their place in His kingdom plan – yet also promising His continued presence. At the beginning of Joshua chapter 1, Moses has just died, and the Lord commissions Joshua to take on the leadership mantle, yet twice within the first chapter, the Lord assures Joshua that, 'I will be with you' (vv5,9).

As those who have received the Lord's Great Commission today, we too are called to 'step out', to take our place in God's kingdom plan to 'make disciples... teaching them to obey everything that [the Lord has commanded]' (vv19–20). Yet, like Joshua, we also have the Lord's promised presence (v20). Whatever the specific challenges of the task ahead, we can be encouraged knowing that the God of Joshua abides with us too, as we embark on His mission within the context He has placed us.

SCRIPTURE TO CONSIDER: Exod. 3:1–12; Josh. 1:1–18; Num. 6:22–27; John 14:15–21

AN ACTION TO TAKE: Bring your day-to-day challenges before the Lord – invite Him into those situations, confident that He goes before you in each situation.

A PRAYER TO MAKE: 'Lord, thank You that You go before us. Help us to trust You as we face new challenges and situations. Amen.'

Mark 1:14–18

'As Jesus walked beside the Sea of Galilee, he saw Simon and his brother Andrew casting a net into the lake, for they were fishermen. "Come, follow me," Jesus said, "and I will send you out to fish for people."' (v17)

The first chapter of Mark reveals the calling of the very first disciples, including Simon and Andrew, two brothers. Their call to be disciples was not a simple bolt-on to an already busy schedule but was to involve three clear aspects.

Firstly, they were called to change their life's direction and follow Jesus (v17). Second, it would involve personal transformation, where Jesus would make them into something (v17). Thirdly, their focus would be God's kingdom project, as they were called to 'fish for people' (v17).

This single verse in Mark chapter 1, neatly summarises what is to be our experience as followers of Christ today. Our call to Christ is not simply a call to personal salvation, as wonderful as that is, but is a call to become a fully allegiant follower of King Jesus, our new Master. This calling involves repentance, turning around from our own ways and direction, and turning to His.

Like Simon and Andrew, our calling will also involve transformation, allowing the Holy Spirit to do His work within us (Rom. 12:2). Finally, it will involve become participants in His grand kingdom project, representing Christ as willing ambassadors (2 Cor. 5:20).

SCRIPTURE TO CONSIDER: Gen. 12:1–6; Exod. 3:1–14; Matt. 7:15–23; Acts 9:1–19

AN ACTION TO TAKE: Think about your day-to-day faith. Is your desire to follow the Lord's lead, to allow Him to change you and use you for His kingdom purposes?

A PRAYER TO MAKE: 'Lord, thank You that You have saved me for a purpose: to follow You, to learn from You and to serve You. Amen.'

Matthew 4:23–25
'Jesus went throughout Galilee, teaching in their synagogues, proclaiming the good news of the kingdom, and healing every disease and sickness among the people. News about him spread all over Syria… Large crowds from Galilee, the Decapolis, Jerusalem, Judea and the region across the Jordan followed him.' (vv23–25)

At the beginning of His ministry the Gospels tell us that Jesus began to teach, 'proclaiming the good news of the kingdom' (v23). In addition, in line with Old Testament prophecies about the signs of the incoming kingdom reign of God (Isa. 58:6; 61:1–2), people were being healed from various diseases, pain and demon-possession (v24). The radical teaching of Jesus, accompanied by the miraculous healings, soon attracted a crowd.

As disciples of Jesus, we find ourselves in various discipleship spaces, each giving us an opportunity to communicate something of the Gospel and God's kingdom. The 'crowds' we find ourselves communicating with represent a 'come and see' opportunity for many. Perhaps this might be a Sunday morning church service, or a regular group we help lead. Maybe it is something less formal such as the 'crowd' at the school gates, or those we connect with at the local gymnasium or running club. These 'come and see' spaces give us opportunity to publicly share or show our faith and point people to Jesus.

Let us each ask the Lord to help us make use of the 'come and see' spaces He has placed us, asking Him to give us insight and wisdom as we seek to represent Him.

SCRIPTURE TO CONSIDER: Josh. 24:1–28; 2 Kgs 23:1–25; Luke 8:16–18; John 4:1–30

AN ACTION TO TAKE: Think about your 'come and see' spaces. Where you can demonstrate your faith in Christ either in word or deed or both.

A PRAYER TO MAKE: 'Lord, thank You that You place us in various contexts that we might point people to You. Amen.'

Mark 8:34–38
'Then he called the crowd to him along with his disciples
and said: "Whoever wants to be my disciple must deny
themselves and take up their cross and follow me. For whoever
wants to save their life will lose it, but whoever loses their
life for me and for the gospel will save it."' (vv34–35)

Beyond Jesus' ministry to the crowds, there were those who were called to 'come and follow'. Some were directly called, like Simon and Andrew (Mark 1:17), others sought Jesus out, like Zacchaeus (Luke 19:1–10). This group of people represent those whose interest and enquiries move beyond general interest. Within our passage of Scripture today, Jesus highlights another level of 'following', what it really takes to be His disciple – one who denies themself, is willing to pay the cost of being a disciple and prioritise the Lord's leading (v34).

We too can seek out those from the 'crowd', perhaps those who have an extra question, or perhaps their own stories of a previous faith encounter. This is more likely to be a smaller group, a few. If we are going to work in this 'come and follow' space, we need to be prepared to give time to this group. It can be easy to focus on the crowd and the large events – yet it is only as we share with a focused group of people, that disciples can start to be formed.

At the same time, it is important that we communicate what it means to love and follow Jesus, including the cost - allowing the Holy Spirit to show us those in the crowd who have an enquiring spirit that are seeking to know more.

SCRIPTURE TO CONSIDER: Judg. 7:1–8; Dan. 5:1–30; Matt. 5:1–12; Luke 19:1–10

AN ACTION TO TAKE: Think about your 'come and follow' spaces. Who are the 'twelve' that the Lord may have placed in your life, those with a deeper enquiry, demonstrating a keener interest?

A PRAYER TO MAKE: 'Lord Jesus, help me not to be distracted by the crowd – and to see those You are leading me to encourage to walk alongside You. Amen.'

Come and Be with Me

Luke 9:28–36
'About eight days after Jesus said this, he took Peter, John and James with him and went up onto a mountain to pray. As he was praying, the appearance of his face changed, and his clothes became as bright as a flash of lightning. Two men, Moses and Elijah, appeared in glorious splendour, talking with Jesus.' (vv28–30)

In our reading today, we see Jesus inviting Peter, James and John into His 'come and be with me' space. As the fulfilment of the law and the prophets, Moses and Elijah appeared alongside Jesus, where Jesus was suddenly transformed so that 'his clothes became as bright as a flash of lightning' (v29). Such was the experience that Peter wanted to remain in this 'space' (v33).

Whilst there were many who preferred to stay in the crowd and simply seek blessing, be that healing or other – others, like Peter, James and John wanted to spend time *with* Jesus – allowing His words and actions to shape them. This model of discipleship, of following, is something for God's people to emulate today – not only as we seek to 'be with Jesus' everyday ourselves – but as we seek to pass on to others what it means to follow Him.

As those called to make disciples, if we allow people to walk alongside us in our daily lives, this allows us to show what following Jesus looks like in the 'everyday'. This could be called our 'come and be with me' space, as we allow people to be up close and personal, seeing how we handle various situations, and our passion for prayer and Scripture. It can be easy for us to keep people at a distance, but it is in the more intimate spaces that we can start to encourage people into a deeper walk with Christ.

SCRIPTURE TO CONSIDER: Gen. 5:21–24; Acts 18:18–28; 2 Thess. 3:6–10; Heb. 6:1–12

AN ACTION TO TAKE: Think about your 'come and be with me' space. Who are the 'three' that the Lord may have placed in your life, those you might spend more time with, demonstrating what following and loving Jesus looks like?

A PRAYER TO MAKE: 'Lord Jesus, help me to make myself vulnerable and open up my life to help others love and follow You. Amen.'

Come and Remain

John 15:1–8

'I am the vine; you are the branches. If you remain in me and I in you, you will bear much fruit; apart from me you can do nothing.' (v5)

A hidden danger of discipleship is that as someone who disciples others, we can think we are the ones that should have all the answers or, as someone being discipled, we can look to the person helping or spiritually guiding us to give us the answers. Either sort of dependency is unhelpful and unscriptural. The ideal 'space' we all need to be in, is one of complete intimacy and dependency on the Lord.

In our reading today, Jesus speaks of a 'come and remain' space, describing this as a 'fruitful' space. Indeed, to emphasise the essential nature of this space, Jesus tells us that 'apart from me, you can do nothing' (v5b). The ultimate aim of discipleship is for us and those we spiritually encourage to dwell in this 'remain' space with Christ, in order that we might bear fruit for the kingdom. All our service, all our relationships should be carried out and developed with this in mind. Over reliance on the Church, or other people can make us fruitless, 'like a branch that is thrown away and withers' (v6a).

It can be easy for us to lose our focus and purpose as God's people – forgetting Christ's call to make disciples. Yet this is not about encouraging people to follow us – but to follow Christ, to enter into that deep, 'remain space' with Him – that they may be able to not only stand firm in life's trials – but be fruitful for His Kingdom.

SCRIPTURE TO CONSIDER: Deut. 4:1–14; 2 Chron. 17:1–19; Gal. 5:13–26; Heb. 4:14–16

AN ACTION TO TAKE: How are we nurturing our own intimacy with Christ and how are we encouraging others to do the same?

A PRAYER TO MAKE: 'Lord Jesus, help me to enter that "remain space" with You – and to encourage others to do the same. Amen.'

Genesis 12:1–5

'The LORD had said to Abram, "Go from your country, your people and your father's household to the land I will show you. I will make you into a great nation, and I will bless you; I will make your name great, and you will be a blessing. I will bless those who bless you, and whoever curses you I will curse; and all peoples on earth will be blessed through you."' (vv1–3)

God's call to discipleship is not a New Testament phenomenon. God has always called a people to Himself, yet not simply to personally follow, but to participate in His redemptive kingdom plan for humanity. In our reading today, we hear of Abram, later to be renamed by the Lord, Abraham, being personally called, yet into an international project. The Lord personally calls Abraham to 'Go... to the land I will show you' (v1), with the bigger redemptive picture being that 'all peoples on earth will be blessed through you' (v3b).

Likewise, our call today is both personal and international. In Matthew chapter 28, verse 19, we are told to personally 'go and make disciples of all nations'. Each of us is challenged to respond to God's call on our lives, whilst always keeping in mind the bigger picture. It can be easy when speaking about our relationship with God to simply speak in personal terms about 'my relationship with the Lord', or 'my personal walk with Jesus'. Now, whilst a personal encounter with Christ must always be our starting point, it is always with the view of taking our place in His kingdom project.

SCRIPTURE TO CONSIDER: Gen. 26:1–6; Josh. 1:1–9; Matt. 28:19–20; Rev. 11:15–19

AN ACTION TO TAKE: What balance are we giving to our personal daily walk with Jesus and His calling on our lives to take our place in His kingdom plan?

A PRAYER TO MAKE: 'Lord Jesus, thank You that You call me personally to walk with You. Help me to see how I might play my part in Your bigger purposes. Amen.'

How Faith Works

Galatians 3:1–9

'Understand, then, that those who have faith are children of Abraham. Scripture foresaw that God would justify the Gentiles by faith, and announced the gospel in advance to Abraham: "All nations will be blessed through you." So those who rely on faith are blessed along with Abraham, the man of faith.' (vv7–9)

When the apostle Paul preached the gospel within the Galatian church, there were some who were concerned that Paul was preaching a 'new gospel'. This caused some to criticise Paul and to slide back into their old, legalistic, religious ways. Yet within our reading today, Paul is keen to demonstrate that whilst the covenantal focus is now different, focused on and fulfilled in Christ, 'How faith works' is the same as it always has been. To demonstrate this, Paul uses Abraham as an example of one who heard God's personal call, who heard the details of God's covenant promise, and responded in obedient faith (see Gen. 15:1–6). As a result of Abraham's obedient response, Paul tells the Galatians that the Lord 'credited to him... righteousness' (v6).

Likewise, this is how faith works today. God personally calls us, He lays out the details of His covenant, fulfilled in Christ at the cross. We are then called to respond in obedient faith as we put our trust in Christ's finished work and ongoing transforming power (see Rom. 12:2). This is not a new gospel but is always the way that the Lord has called His people to Himself. Our response is to lean on, to put our faith in, His covenant promise – knowing as we do so that we too, like Abraham, are justified by faith (v8).

SCRIPTURE TO CONSIDER: Gen. 15:1–6; Matt. 7:24–29; Rom. 3:21–31; Heb. 11:1–40

AN ACTION TO TAKE: How are we demonstrating our faith in action?

A PRAYER TO MAKE: 'Lord God, thank You that Your Word comes to us, calls us, and challenges us to faithful obedience. Amen.'

The Rock of Obedience

Matthew 7:24–29

'Therefore everyone who hears these words of mine and puts them into practice is like a wise man who built his house on the rock. The rain came down, the streams rose, and the winds blew and beat against that house; yet it did not fall, because it had its foundation on the rock.' (vv24–25)

The act of following Christ is exercised through obedience. This is demonstrated in a familiar, yet often misinterpreted parable that Jesus told about the wise and foolish builders. Within this parable in Matthew chapter 7 (also found in Luke 6:46–49), Jesus speaks of two men, one who built his house upon sand, the other on the rock. Traditionally, many people interpret the rock to be Jesus. Although building lives on and around Christ is of course central to the Christian walk, in this parable Jesus was speaking about a very specific aspect of our daily response to Him and His Word. The clue is in the words, 'everyone who hears these words of mine and puts them into practice' (v24), or to paraphrase, 'whoever hears these words of mine and responds in obedience'. The rock in this parable, is the rock of obedience.

Reading *Every Day with Jesus*, and particularly the related scriptures, brings both encouragement and challenge to our daily lives. Yet if it changes very little of what we do or how we approach life, then we are like the man who built his house upon the sand of disobedience, vulnerable in life's storms. Yet, as we respond in willing obedience, even as we stumble and fall, we can have confidence that we will stand firm through the challenges of life, standing on the rock of obedience.

SCRIPTURE TO CONSIDER: Exod. 19:1–6; Deut. 6:1–25; Ps. 119:1–8; Luke 11:14–28

AN ACTION TO TAKE: How is our love for God's Word being demonstrated in obedient service?

A PRAYER TO MAKE: 'Lord God, thank You that You call us to serve You faithfully. Help us to follow You in loving obedience. Amen.'

Riches Versus Cost

Luke 18:18–30
'Jesus looked at him and said, "How hard it is for the rich to enter the kingdom of God!"' (v24)

L uke chapter 18 reveals an encounter between Jesus and a wealthy young man. Like many biblical stories, various emphases have been placed on this interaction, ranging from the barrier of wealth to spiritual matters, through to consideration and care for the poor. Whilst each of these extremes is not wrong per se, it can be easy for us to miss the gospel writer's increasing emphasis on the cost of following Jesus.

Each gospel has an intentional flow of stories and accounts that are designed to challenge our priorities and encourage us to a new kingdom focus. Whilst the disciples in our text today are focused on the riches of the young man (v26), Jesus focuses their attention on cost (v29).

A mind focused on riches, uses language of acquisition, receiving, even personal blessing. A cost focused mind focuses on serving, sacrifice, giving. Life can be tough, with many and varied challenges, so it can be natural to focus our attention and prayers on our needs and circumstances. Yet, increasingly, in a broken world, God's people are called to demonstrate a better way, a kingdom way, that seeks God's kingdom first (Matt. 6:33).

Jesus never shied away from spelling out the cost of following Him (Mark 8:34-28) - neither should we.

SCRIPTURE TO CONSIDER: Prov. 4:1–9; Matt. 6:25–34; Luke 14:25–35; 1 Cor. 3:1–23

AN ACTION TO TAKE: In what sense do we focus on the riches of receiving and blessing, yet ignore the cost of God's call on our lives?

A PRAYER TO MAKE: 'Lord God, help me to be willing to count the cost of following You. Amen.'

Genesis 22:1–19

'The angel of the LORD called to Abraham from heaven a second time and said, "I swear by myself, declares the LORD, that because you have done this and have not withheld your son, your only son, I will surely bless you and make your descendants as numerous as the stars in the sky and as the sand on the seashore."' (vv15–17)

The sacrifice that each of us might be asked to give in our service for God will be different, it will be personal. Cost and sacrifice are something we feel. For Abraham, the most precious thing to him was his son, a child he had waited years for, long promised by the Lord Himself (Gen. 15:4). So, as his promised heir, it would have seemed baffling to Abraham that the Lord would ask him to give up Isaac by way of sacrifice. Yet in a bizarre twist of events in Genesis chapter 22, as Abraham prepares to obediently carry out the Lord's instructions, the Lord Himself, seeing Abraham's willingness, provides a substitute in the form of a ram (v13). Abraham's willingness to entrust even the most precious thing to the Lord, revealed his sacrificial heart of service.

We can often cling onto things that are precious to us, unwilling to allow God to have complete lordship over our lives. Perhaps our finances, relationships or career plans. The important thing for all of us is not that we necessarily have to give up everything that is precious to us, but that we have a sacrificial heart that is willing to do so. Whatever sacrifice we may or may not be asked to give, it can never compare to the ultimate sacrifice God Himself has made, in giving us His precious Son Jesus.

SCRIPTURE TO CONSIDER: Gen. 15:1–21; 1 Sam. 15:1–35; Heb. 11:17–19; 1 John 4:7–21

AN ACTION TO TAKE: What areas of our lives might we be clinging onto, refusing to allow Christ's lordship?

A PRAYER TO MAKE: 'Lord Jesus, help me to be willing to give every area of my life over to You. Amen.'

1 John 4:7–21

'Dear friends, let us love one another, for love comes from God. Everyone who loves has been born of God and knows God. Whoever does not love does not know God, because God is love.' (vv7–8)

Serving the Lord is a great privilege, yet also a great responsibility. It can be easy after or even during a long season of service to start to feel weary or even resentful. Yet in our text today, John reveals where both our strength and motivation for service come from. Verse 7 tells us 'love comes from God'. This is our strength for service, with verse 10 telling us, 'This is love, not that we loved God, but that He loved us and sent His Son as an atoning sacrifice for our sins' – this is our motivation for service. Our very capacity to love comes from God, and it is Him that gives us the supreme example of what total love looks like, as we gaze at the cross.

Keeping in mind God's empowering love and His commitment to us, demonstrated at the cross, helps us to keep perspective during times of trial, weakness and life's general challenges. The apostle Paul, to the Galatian church says, 'Let us not become weary in doing good, for at the proper time we will reap a harvest if we do not give up' (Gal. 6:9).

However weary or discouraged we may get from time to time, it is helpful to focus on His all-embracing, all-empowering love – remembering that He 'went first', He first loved us.

Love so amazing so divine, demands my soul, my life, my all.*

SCRIPTURE TO CONSIDER: Ps. 102:1–28; Isa. 40:1–31; Gal. 6:1–10; Col. 1:1–13

AN ACTION TO TAKE: Take time to rest and to ponder God's great love for you – allow this to motivate you to keep serving as He strengthens you.

A PRAYER TO MAKE: 'Lord, may Your love continually strengthen me and motivate me to serve You. Amen.'

*Isaac Watts, 1707

Lifted Up

Isaiah 40:1–31

'He gives strength to the weary and increases the power of the weak. Even youths grow tired and weary, and young men stumble and fall; but those who hope in the LORD will renew their strength. They will soar on wings like eagles; they will run and not grow weary, they will walk and not be faint.' (vv29–31)

Many believers find themselves in a place of discouragement, perhaps weary from criticism, seeing little fruit for their labours, or struggling with past failures and guilt. In our text today from Isaiah chapter 40, the Lord wants to encourage His despondent people. He does this by giving them two perspectives. One is a realistic view of themselves, the other is a realistic view of just who He is. These two perspectives are also important for us to keep in mind. A skewed vision of ourselves might lead to over-confidence in our own abilities, a skewed vision of God can lead to doubt and despondency.

Isaiah 40 tells us several things about ourselves – we are imperfect and sinful (vv1–2), frail (vv6–7), and our knowledge of God is limited (vv12–14). Yet, in comparison, the Lord consoles us and deals with our sin (vv1–2), He is glorious (v5), His Word is enduring (v8), He is Sovereign (v10), He carries us close to His heart (v11), He is unfathomable (v13), incomparable (v18), all-powerful (vv21–24), and eternal (v28). Ultimately, we can be encouraged that it is this God that renews our strength and lifts us up (v31).

SCRIPTURE TO CONSIDER: Ps. 29:1–11 & 37:1–40; Isa. 41:1–10; Phil. 4:1–13

AN ACTION TO TAKE: Ponder the character of God revealed in Isaiah 40. Commit your way to Him.

A PRAYER TO MAKE: 'Lord, give me a true perspective of who I am and who You are. May I depend on You in all situations. Amen.'

Looking Up

Psalm 121:1–8

'I lift up my eyes to the mountains – where does my help come from? My help comes from the LORD, the Maker of heaven and earth. He will not let your foot slip – he who watches over you will not slumber; indeed, he who watches over Israel will neither slumber nor sleep..' (vv1–4)

As we enter this season of Advent, building up to the celebration of the birth of our Lord and Saviour, Jesus Christ, it could be easy for us to be distracted by the season's celebrations and the expectations of others. Within our Advent considerations, we want to encourage focus on the expectations and hope found in looking to God.

This expectation and hope are captured in Psalm 121, as the writer encourages us to 'look up' to our Helper and Maker (vv1–2). So often we look around us at the varying demands on our time, or look down in despair, with this time of year being a time of sadness and loneliness for many – perhaps missing loved ones, or feeling friendless. We may even look behind us at past regrets and mistakes.

However, our expectation and hope come as we look upwards – to the One who watches over us (v3), and who guides and protects us (vv5–8). This Advent season, where we look matters. As we look to God, He can change our sadness to celebration, our helplessness to hope, our despair to expectation.

At the same time, we can encourage others, overwhelmed by their day to day, to look up to Him too.

SCRIPTURE TO CONSIDER: Ps. 130:1–8; Isa. 9:1–7; Luke 2:22–32 & 21:5–28

AN ACTION TO TAKE: In which direction do you look as a rule? Look up to God's promises and thank Him for this season of expectation and hope.

A PRAYER TO MAKE: 'Lord, help me to lift my eyes to You, the Lord the Maker of heaven and earth. Amen.'

Little Samuels

1 Samuel 3:1–21

'The boy Samuel ministered before the LORD under Eli. In those days the word of the LORD was rare; there were not many visions.' (v1)

Arguably, the start of 1 Samuel reflects one of the darkest and most depressing spiritual periods of God's people found in Scripture. Commencing with a story of physical barrenness (chapter 1), chapter 3 depicts a season of spiritual barrenness and darkness. Spiritual darkness is one thing, yet a silent darkness is another – 'the Word of the Lord was rare'. On top of this, the clergy were also fraudulent, with Eli indifferent to his sons' rebellion and abuse of their office (v13). Yet even here, encouragement is offered as verse 1 tells us, 'The boy Samuel ministered before the Lord...' Even in the midst of this bleak chapter, the Lord is at work in and through a little boy called Samuel.

The Advent season reminds us that God brings hope into despair, light into darkness. We too might find ourselves in a dark chapter of faith and following. It can be easy to be overwhelmed by life's events and circumstances, with perhaps even God Himself seeming distant and silent. Yet we too can look for the 'little Samuels', for the ways God is still at work – working His purposes out in spite of, not because of, us. As the chorus says, He is our 'Way maker, miracle worker, promise keeper, light in the darkness'.*

Whatever we are facing at the moment - let us look for the 'little Samuels' of God's providence and care.

SCRIPTURE TO CONSIDER: Gen. 1:1–3; Isa. 53:1–12; Matt. 4:12–17; John 1:1–13

AN ACTION TO TAKE: Let's ask ourselves: How do we see the Lord working in our lives, even in the smallest ways?

A PRAYER TO MAKE: 'Lord, help me to see how You are working – even when all around seems dark. Amen.'

*Sinach, 2015.

Genesis 3:1–24
'So the LORD God said to the snake, "Because you have done this, 'Cursed are you above all livestock and all wild animals! You will crawl on your belly and you will eat dust all the days of your life. And I will put enmity between you and the woman, and between your offspring and hers; he will crush your head, and you will strike his heel."' (vv14–15)

Knowing the story we are part of is so important. It can be easy to get caught up in the single chapters of both life's challenges and adventures. Yet keeping in mind the bigger picture can help us as we seek to make sense of our part in it. Genesis 3 reveals the introduction of sin into the world, and its consequences, with work and family life becoming more laboured and challenging (vv16–19). Yet, within this chapter, we are also given a glimpse of hope and of God's bigger redemptive story, as verse 15 foretells the future defeat of Satan, sin and all that the serpent represents (v15b).

Advent reminds us of the fulfilment of this verse as we celebrate the birth of Jesus, the One who would 'crush the serpent's head'. Subsequently, Jesus' life, death, resurrection and ultimate return 'reverse the curse' of Genesis 3. Keeping the big story in mind helps us to keep perspective, and so, as God's people, we can now celebrate all that Christ has achieved for us, knowing that whatever life chapter we may be facing right now, in the end 'we win'.

God is working His purpose out, As year gives way to year
God is working His purpose out, And the tide is drawing near
Near and nearer draws the time, The time that will surely be
When the earth will be filled with the glory of God, As the waters
cover the sea*

SCRIPTURE TO CONSIDER: 2 Sam. 7:1–17; Ps. 107:1–43; Isa. 55:1–13; Acts 2:14–41

AN ACTION TO TAKE: Think about how you would communicate the big story of the Bible.

A PRAYER TO MAKE: 'Lord, thank You that You have a big story and that You call me to live in the light of it. Amen.'
*AC Ainger, 1894

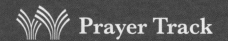
WELCOME TO PRAYER TRACK, offering you key prayer points each week to help you join hundreds of others in praying for the world, our Christian family worldwide and issues closer to home.

31 OCT – 6 NOV COPING WITH CHANGE

"Do not be anxious about anything, but in every situation, by prayer and petition, with thanksgiving, present your requests to God" Philippians 4:6

- As seasons change we're reminded that adapting to change can be tough. Pray for people you know in a season of change. Pray for comfort and guidance as they adapt to change.

- Pray for people who struggle with Seasonal Affective Disorder during the shorter days. Pray for their energy-levels and ways to boost their mood.

- Thank God for Firework Displays this week! Pray that these events will inspire togetherness in the community and bring joy and fun on dark nights.

- If you're struggling with change, God wants to hear about it. Let Him know what's in your heart and pray for peace that transcends understanding.

WEEKEND

Father God – while change is inevitable, it's not always easy. We pray for those people adapting to a significant change in their lives and pray that they'll know Your presence all the more this week. Amen.

7 – 13 NOV REMEMBERANCE

"I will remember the deeds of the Lord; yes, I will remember your wonders of old." Psalm 77:11

- If you're in a season of processing loss or grief, take a moment to remember, and thank God for the gift you had at that time.

- Remember God is leading, even when you walk through the wilderness. Thank God that He's by your side, always.

- Pray for the families that lost a loved one who served in the armed forces. Pray for comfort as they remember them during special services on Sunday.

- Look back over the last week, month or year, and remember the ways God has been good. Thank God for His good gifts, which give us hope.

WEEKEND

Lord Jesus – as we look towards Remembrance Sunday, we remember those who fought and died in war. We remember your own sacrifice on the cross for all of us. Thank you for your courage, selflessness and love. Amen.

14 – 20 NOV PRAISE

"And all the people gave a great shout of praise to the Lord, because the foundation of the house of the Lord was laid." Ezra 3:11

- Thank God for the bright minds who think up creative and innovative technology to combat climate change. Pray for more ideas and funding and for the success of these projects.

- Thank God for the counsellors of this world, who bring healing to so many.

- Thank the Lord for the compassionate and hardworking staff who make up the NHS and the care sector.

- Jesus – thank you for the peacemakers of this world, who follow your example and work for reconciliation. Thank you for their patience and optimism.

- Thank God for the relationships in your life, whether that's friends, family, colleagues, pets. Name them and thank God for your connections.

WEEKEND

Father God – you give us so many good gifts and we acknowledge your goodness in our lives. Thank you for the ways in which you care for us, and the ways in which you're working for the good of the world.

21 – 27 NOV   **WORLD FOCUS**

"God's people should make petitions, prayers, intercessions and thanksgivings on behalf of all people" 1 Timothy 2:1

- **Ukraine:** Pray for an end to the war in Ukraine. Lift up Volodymyr Zelenesky and pray for his resilience, and continued leadership of the country.

- **Taiwan:** Pray for the tension with China to dissipate and pray for their protection against invasion.

- **Afghanistan:** There are around 2 million refugees and asylum seekers from Afghanistan and an additional 3.4 million internally displace persons in the country. Pray for the safety and wellbeing and pray for stability in the country so that it is restored to a place where people want to live again.

- **Syria:** There is a continued political and socio-economic crisis that has resulted in a severe deterioration in living conditions. Pray for funding and people with healthcare expertise to reach the country for urgent provision of healthcare. Pray for provision, malnourished and access to safe water, especially for those who are displaced.

WEEKEND

Father God – we pray for people around the world who struggle in war-torn countries. We pray for an end to war and we pray for restoration and recovery for those who have suffered. Lord, we know your heart breaks for these situations. Help us to do what we can to bring about Your will on earth. Amen.

28 Nov – 4 DEC   **ADVENT**

"How beautiful on the mountains are the feet of those who bring good news, who proclaim peace, who bring good tidings, who proclaim salvation, who say to Zion "Your God reigns!"" Isaiah 52:7

- As we begin Advent this week, ask God to prepare your heart for the season; to be someone who carries peace as we approach Christmas

- Pray for the preparations in churches nationwide. Pray for the energy levels of church staff and that all the planning for carol services and Christmas services goes smoothly.

- These weeks leading up to Christmas can feel hectic with all the preparations. Ask God for moments of calm and pray to stay tuned in to His voice, His peace and His love for you.

- Thank God for the hope you have, and pray that you'll find ways this week to bring that hope to others.

- Pray for your church this Advent; for great relationships within the congregation and for newcomers to feel welcome and settle in quickly.

5 – 11 DEC   DISCIPLESHIP

"Therefore go and make disciples of all nations, baptising them in the name of the Father and of the Son and of the Holy Spirit, and teaching them to obey everything I have commanded you. And surely I am with you always, to the very end of the age." Matthew 28:18-20

- Pray for discipleship to flourish in our churches, so that empowered disciples can effect change in contemporary culture.

- Pray for your own practise of discipleship. Ask God how you can follow Christ more closely this week.

- As disciples, we are called to 'love one another'. Ask the Holy Spirit to call to mind anyone who particularly needs your love this week and think of a way to bless them.

- Pray Christ's disciples throughout the world will fulfil the Great Commission to make disciples of all men.

- Thank God for His goodness and faithfulness in your discipleship journey. Remember He smiles on you as His child and He is proud of you.

12 – 18 DEC   LOCAL COMMUNITY

"And we urge you, brothers and sisters, warn those who are idle and disruptive, encourage the disheartened, help the weak, be patient with everyone." 1 Thessalonians 4:14

- Pray for your local community in the build up to Christmas. Pray for those who feel isolated or excluded from the festivities. Pray that they'll find inclusion.

- Pray for your local church ministry; that people on outreach missions will find the people that need their help the most.

- Pray for an end to homelessness in your local community. It's a complex problem, but nothing is too big for God. Pray that He will intervene with the right people, and the right care to provide stability, safety and shelter.

- Pray for joy to overflow in your community and that your relationships with neighbours and friends will flourish.

- Remember that you carry God's Holy Spirit and pray for a greater awareness of those 'small still voice' promptings this week to encourage your local community

19 – 25 DEC   **CHRISTMAS**

"For God so loved the world, that He gave His only Son, that whoever believes in Him should not perish but have eternal life." John 3:16

- In this final week before Christmas, we pray that the week will be characterised by joy. Pray for families coming together and for fun and unity.

- Pray for those people who find Christmas difficult. Pray that they'll be blessed this year with companionship, compassion and understanding.

- Pray for people responsible for cooking Christmas dinner! Pray that the preparation will be filled with fun and laughter rather than stress.

- Pray that more and more people will feel and understand God's love for us as we share gifts with each other. God always wants to give us good gifts.

- Thank God for the gift of Jesus on the first Christmas Day.

26 DEC – 1 JAN   **NEW YEAR**

"On account of his vast mercy, he has given us new birth. You have been born anew into a living hope through the resurrection of Jesus Christ from the dead." — 1 Peter 1:3

- As we move into a new year, take time to reflect on the year that's just passed. Thank God that He journeyed with you.

- Commit this year to God and pray for renewed adventures in faith this year.

- Be still and listen for a word from God. Maybe it's a verse, or a word of hope. Ask to hear God's words for next year.

- Clothe yourself with the full armour of God for the year and pray for strength in the Lord for 2023.

- Pray that 2023 is a year of breakthrough, either personal or on global issues like climate change, the cost of living, and peace-keeping.

waverleyabbeytrust.org

Tel: 01252 784700
Email: info@waverleyabbey.org

We would love to keep you up to date on all aspects of the ministry, including new books, courses, events and how you can support us. Update your preferences any time by contacting Customer Services on 01252 784700. You can view our privacy policy on our website.

Romans 5:1–5

'And hope does not put us to shame, because God's love has been poured out into our hearts through the Holy Spirit, who has been given to us.' (v5)

The season of Advent heralds hope. It speaks of God becoming flesh and breaking into this dark world (John 1:14). It speaks of words of promise breaking a long silence between the testaments (Luke 1:26–33). It speaks of the fulfilment of redemptive prophecy (Luke 1:54–55). This is not a vague or faint hope that something *might* happen; it is a certain hope based on the promises of God (Heb. 11:1).

What is more, God is not stingy with His hope, but He literally has 'poured [it] into our hearts' (v5).

Perhaps in the coming Christmas season we might hope for many things: family get togethers, a special gift, or time out from the day-to-day stresses of our everyday work. These things may or may not happen, and may fulfil all that we expected them to do, or not. However, the promises of God, fulfilled in Christ, give us a sure and certain hope that we can lean on, rely on, put our faith in – Jesus is our certain hope. Whatever we might be hoping for this Christmas time, may we look to the One who is able to give us a fulfilled life and who, ultimately, as Romans chapter five tells us, gives us 'peace with God' (v1).

In addition, may we also use this season of hope to lavishly 'pour out' this hope to others who are seeking encouragement and answers in this challenging world.

SCRIPTURE TO CONSIDER: Ps. 25:1–22 & 33:1–22; Isa. 22:8–26; Titus 2:1–15

AN ACTION TO TAKE: Think about where your hope lies today.

A PRAYER TO MAKE: 'Lord, thank You that those who hope in You will renew their strength and that hope in You is certain and sure. Amen.'

Luke 1:5–25

'Zechariah asked the angel, "How can I be sure of this? I am an old man and my wife is well on in years." The angel said to him, "I am Gabriel. I stand in the presence of God, and I have been sent to speak to you and to tell you this good news. And now you will be silent and not able to speak until the day this happens, because you did not believe my words, which will come true at their appointed time."' (vv18–20)

Zechariah was a priest who loved God's Word and God's things. Luke tells us that both Zechariah and his wife Elizabeth were righteous and blameless people before God (v6). Yet when the angel Gabriel appeared to Zechariah to announce that his wife was pregnant, he struggled to believe it (v18). As a consequence of his disbelief, Zechariah was temporarily unable to speak (v20).

Like Zechariah, we too can become familiar with the things of God yet fail to allow the reality and enormity of the truths of God's Word to sink in and impact our lives. Christmas is one such time when we speak and hear about a story familiar to many of us. Yet it can be easy for us to lose the wonder and amazement of this Advent season, perhaps even weary of hearing some of the same carols and stories at this time of year. As we think about the Christmas story, God Himself becoming flesh, breaking into history, our Lord and Saviour reversing the curse of sin and death – may we never lose the awe of this Christmas season. The hymn exhorts us to sing:

> Joy to the world, the Lord is come,
> Let earth receive her King.
> Let every heart prepare Him room,
> And heaven and nature sing.*

SCRIPTURE TO CONSIDER: Isa. 7:13–17; Mic. 5:1–15; Matt. 1:18–25; Luke 1:46–56

AN ACTION TO TAKE: Ponder the wonder of the Christmas story. Think about how you might share this with someone.

A PRAYER TO MAKE: 'Lord, may I never lose the wonder of Christmas. Help me to celebrate this season with freshness. Amen.'

*Isaac Watts, 1719.

Luke 1:46–56
**'And Mary said: "My soul glorifies the Lord and my spirit
rejoices in God my Saviour, for he has been mindful of the
humble state of his servant. From now on all generations
will call me blessed, for the Mighty One has done great
things for me – holy is his name."' (vv46–49)**

When the full realisation and enormity of the angel Gabriel's
announcement sank in for Mary, that she would give birth to
the long-promised Saviour, her reaction was one of praise and
rejoicing. In what is titled 'Mary's song' in Scripture, the lyrics give us
a great model for our worship as we celebrate the birth of Christ today.
Mary's song glorified the Lord (v46) and acknowledged Him as Saviour
(v47). The wonder of God with us is also something to pass on to future
generations (v48), pointing people to the great things God has done (v49).

Many people today lament the sense of what they see as a loss of
the Christmas spirit – often commenting on how it 'does not feel like
Christmas'. Yet, like Mary, as God's people, we have something to sing
about. Might it be as we celebrate Christmas this year, that we are able
to point those around us to the Saviour, singing of His wonderful acts and
glorifying Him.

    I will sing the wondrous story
    Of the Christ who died for me
    How He left His home in glory
    For the cross of Calvary.

SCRIPTURE TO CONSIDER: 2 Sam. 22:1–51; Ps. 28:1–9 & 149:1–9; Col. 3:15–17

AN ACTION TO TAKE: Think about a favourite Christmas song or carol. Share with
someone why it is so special to you.

A PRAYER TO MAKE: 'Lord, thank You that You have put a song in my heart, that I
may point people to You and sing about Your wonders and grace. Amen.'
*F H Rowley (1886)

Out of Small Things

Micah 5:1–15

'But you, Bethlehem Ephrathah, though you are small among the clans of Judah, out of you will come for me one who will be ruler over Israel, whose origins are from of old, from ancient times.' (v2)

In Micah's time, when he was prophesying to Israel, he witnessed great devastation, including the destruction of Israel by Assyria (722BC). Micah's message contains themes of the Lord's judgment (1:2–5), yet also His great faithfulness (6:8), ultimately pointing to the day He would bring One out of Bethlehem, a Messianic ruler (5:2).

Out of this small backwater, Bethlehem, would come a great Saviour. As we celebrate Christmas this year, there are many 'small things' that we can do, that can actually have a great impact.

Perhaps sending a card to someone, letting them know we are thinking of and praying for them. Maybe giving someone a call. So many, especially after the pandemic, crave human contact. Or maybe a simple act of kindness to a stranger or neighbour.

These things, though small to us, can be used by God to bring about great things. Perhaps causing someone to enquire about the true purpose of celebrating Christmas, perhaps someone deciding to attend their local carol service, perhaps someone seeking Jesus, the One promised 'from ancient times'. Small things in God's hands can achieve great outcomes.

SCRIPTURE TO CONSIDER: 1 Kgs 17:7–24; Zech. 4:1–14; Matt. 13:31–35 & 15:29–39

AN ACTION TO TAKE: Think about a small thing that you can do for someone this Christmas.

A PRAYER TO MAKE: 'Lord, thank You that You can take the things I offer You, that may seem small to me, and use them for Your glory and purposes. Amen.'

Repeating Songs

Luke 1:57–80

'Praise be to the Lord, the God of Israel, because he has come to his people and redeemed them. He has raised up a horn of salvation for us in the house of his servant David…' (vv68–69)

Many people love singing their favourite carols and songs at Christmas. As we go about our day-to-day tasks – at home, in the shopping centres – songs of Christmas celebration can often be heard ringing out. Of course, for God's people, the focus should always be on the One in whose name we celebrate Christmas in the first place – Jesus. Christmas is a great opportunity for us to share with those around us why we love this season, and perhaps why a certain carol means so much to us. Indeed, many carols contain great truths of God's love and redemption.

In Luke chapter 1, once Zechariah the priest's voice returned, the first thing he did was sing to the Lord, 'praising God' (v64). Like Mary's song earlier in the chapter, Zechariah's song also reminds us of the great truths we are called to celebrate. He is our redeemer (v68), the source of our salvation (v69), the promised one (v70), our deliverer (v71), a merciful, promise-keeping God (vv72–73), our rescuer (v74) who is holy and righteous (v75). We can easily become over familiar with Christmas carols, perhaps they may even lose their appeal to us. Yet many of the songs we sing at Christmas will contain several of these elements of truth. May we never tire of these 'repeating songs'.

SCRIPTURE TO CONSIDER: Deut. 32:1–4; Ps. 9:1–20 & 30:1–12; Phil. 4:4–9

AN ACTION TO TAKE: Think about a favourite carol – what truths of God does it contain?

A PRAYER TO MAKE: 'Lord, may we never tire of singing your eternal truths. Amen.'

Matthew 2:1–18

'After Jesus was born in Bethlehem in Judea, during the time of King Herod, Magi from the east came to Jerusalem and asked, "Where is the one who has been born king of the Jews? We saw his star when it rose and have come to worship him." When King Herod heard this he was disturbed, and all Jerusalem with him.' (vv1–3)

Despite the excitement of many within the early chapters of Matthew's and Luke's Gospels at the announcement of the birth of Jesus, there were others who were not so excited. Indeed, they were opposed to and felt threatened by the news. King Herod was one such individual. Matthew tells us, 'When King Herod heard [the news] he was disturbed, and all Jerusalem with him' (v3). As a result, Herod set out to extinguish this threat to his reign (v13).

Not everyone shares the excitement of Jesus' birth at Christmas. Whilst some may be opposed to the celebration, even more will be indifferent to the reason Christians celebrate this time of year. Opposition to God's purposes, plans and people is something that has been present from the beginning, fuelled by Satan and his forces (Gen. 3:15). The apostle Paul tells us that our fight is not against flesh and blood but rather is against the evil forces of Satan and his associated principalities (Eph. 6:12).

As we celebrate Christmas, we should not be surprised that there is a counter narrative taking place, an alternative story of denial, greed and self-gratification. All the more reason for us to celebrate openly and unashamedly the wonder of 'God with us'.

SCRIPTURE TO CONSIDER: Gen. 3:1–15; Eph. 6:10–20; 1 Pet. 5:1–10; Rev. 20:7–10

AN ACTION TO TAKE: How might we 'counter' the counter narratives that try to obscure the true purpose of Christmas?

A PRAYER TO MAKE: 'Lord, help me to unashamedly praise You in the places and contexts You have put me. Amen.'

Amazing Gift

2 Corinthians 9:6–15
'And in their prayers for you their hearts will go out to you, because of the surpassing grace God has given you. Thanks be to God for his indescribable gift!' (vv14–15)

It can be nice to both give and receive gifts at Christmas time. Whilst the earthly value of each gift may vary, the important thing is the love and thought that has gone into buying or making it. In his second letter to the Corinthians, the apostle Paul is encouraging the Corinthian church to organise a monetary gift, a collection for their less well-off brothers and sisters in Christ in Jerusalem. To encourage them to be generous, Paul compares their giving with God's, inferring that whatever gift the Corinthians might give, must always be done in the light of God's 'indescribable gift' of Jesus (v15).

Christmas gives us an opportunity, as Christ followers, to be generous in many ways. Perhaps with our time – spending time with others and encouraging them. Perhaps with our gifting – using our skills and gifts to bless others. Perhaps in the giving of a gift – something that says we care and value the receiver. Whatever way we decide to give this Christmas, if we do so in the light of God's gift of Jesus, we will reflect His generous heart and character. We are never more like God than when we give, as John chapter 3, verse 16 tells us: 'For God so loved the world he gave...'

SCRIPTURE TO CONSIDER: Prov. 11:1–31 & 22:1–16; 1 Tim. 6:17–19, Titus 3:1–8

AN ACTION TO TAKE: How might we demonstrate God's generous character this Christmas?

A PRAYER TO MAKE: 'Lord, thank You that You have given us Your very best in Christ. Help me to represent Your giving character this Christmas season. Amen.'

John 1:1–18
**'The light shines in the darkness, and the
darkness has not overcome it.' (v5)**

One of the notable things about Christmas is the enormous array of lights that go on display in shops and streets. In many roads, people can become quite competitive as they seek to 'outshine' their neighbours' displays! Indeed, once Christmas is over and the lights are taken down, the once bright shops, homes and streets can look dull by comparison. John's Gospel starts by telling us about a great 'light' that came into the world that very first Christmas – Jesus. Into this dark world, 'The light [shone]' (v5). Yet this was no ordinary light, this was the Light of life (v4).

As we celebrate Jesus, the Light of the world, we too are called to reflect and point to the Light (v8). In this world of darkness and uncertainty, with rising costs, wars and uprisings, even the smallest light can be visible. In Matthew chapter 5, Jesus tells us, 'You are the light of the world. A town built on a hill cannot be hidden. Neither do people light a lamp and put it under a bowl. Instead, they put it on its stand, and it gives light to everyone in the house. In the same way, let your light shine before others, that they may see your good deeds and glorify your Father in heaven' (vv14–16) May the light of Christ shine through us throughout and beyond the season's celebrations.

This little light of mine, I'm gonna let it shine,
This little light of mine, I'm gonna let it shine,
This little light of mine, I'm gonna let it shine,
everyday, everyday, everyday in every way,
I'm gonna let my little light shine.

Anon.

SCRIPTURE TO CONSIDER: Isa. 60:1–22; Prov. 13:9; Matt. 5:13–16; Phil. 2:12–18

AN ACTION TO TAKE: How might we reflect Christ's light to those around us?

A PRAYER TO MAKE: 'Lord, help me to shine for You in this world of darkness and uncertainty. Amen.'

Seeking Him

Luke 2:1–21

'When the angels had left them and gone into heaven, the shepherds said to one another, "Let's go to Bethlehem and see this thing that has happened, which the Lord has told us about."' (v15)

Luke chapter 2 tells us of another encounter between heaven and earth – angels visiting shepherds tending their flocks in the fields (vv9–12). The good news of the birth of Jesus was not just for wise men, it was for all people – people doing everyday jobs like the shepherds. Luke tells us that once the angels had left them, they wanted to seek Jesus for themselves, 'to go to Bethlehem and see this thing that [had] happened' (v15). Yet once the shepherds found Jesus, they did not keep this great news to themselves, but 'spread the word concerning what had been told them about this child' (v17).

Perhaps we too have heard the good news of Christmas and heard of or know of others who are seeking Jesus and celebrating His birth. The call of Christmas is for all people. Whatever our background, whatever our life's circumstances, Christmas calls each of us to seek Jesus for ourselves, not relying on the stories of others. Then once we have done that, and experienced a personal, life-changing encounter with Him, like the shepherds, we too are called to 'spread the word'.

Perhaps this Christmas, as we go about our daily business in the everyday places that the Lord has called us to serve and represent Him – maybe we can take the opportunity to share with others what God has done, 'this thing that has happened' (v15). May Jesus never be the best kept secret in our lives.

SCRIPTURE TO CONSIDER: Deut. 4:15–30; 1 Chron. 16:8–11; Ps. 40:1–17; Luke 11:1–13

AN ACTION TO TAKE: How are we encouraging others to seek Jesus?

A PRAYER TO MAKE: 'Lord, thank You that those who seek You with all their heart, find You. Amen.'

Ephesians 2:11–22
**'Consequently, you are no longer foreigners and
strangers, but fellow citizens with God's people
and also members of his household…' (v19)**

Christmas can be a stressful time for many people, especially when it comes to family. Whilst some families are close and love to get together to celebrate this season, others find it difficult, perhaps still nursing past hurts, misunderstandings and rejection. It can be easy to focus on our differences, the things that set us apart, instead of those that unite. In his letter to the Ephesians, Paul was writing to a mixed church of Jews and Gentiles who were very different in both their upbringing and culture. These differences had long separated them, something Paul refers to as a 'dividing wall' (v14). Yet, rather than focusing on their differences, Paul encouraged the Ephesian church to focus on what united them – that being their relationship to Christ, describing Jesus as their 'peace' (v14).

If we have the opportunity to gather with family or friends this Christmas, whatever has gone on before, whatever previous hurts have happened, whatever 'dividing wall' there may have been between us, as God's people we can seek to encourage peace through Christ. This may be easier with those who share the same values and interests as us but, as Paul encouraged the Ephesians, with all their differences, let us also seek unity as we point to Christ, the One who has made peace possible.

SCRIPTURE TO CONSIDER: Num. 6:24–26; Psa. 34:1–22 & 122:1–9; Matt. 5:1–12

AN ACTION TO TAKE: What steps might we be able to take to reach out to those who misunderstand us or who have hurt us in the past?

A PRAYER TO MAKE: 'Lord, thank You that You are the ultimate peacemaker. Help me to be an agent of peace this Christmas. Amen.'

Family Tree

Matthew 1:1–16
'...and Jacob the father of Joseph, the husband of Mary, and Mary was the mother of Jesus who is called the Messiah.' (v16)

The start of Matthew's Gospel gives us the genealogy of 'Jesus the Messiah' (v1). This may seem like a strange start to the nativity story, but being able to trace their lineage was important to the predominantly Jewish audience to which Matthew was writing. Matthew traces the family tree of Jesus from Abraham, an important and central figure to the Jewish people.

The family tree of Jesus is both a source of encouragement and challenge for us today. It can be easy to consider the Christmas story as a fairy tale or fable, putting it on our bookshelves alongside other stories such as *Snow White*, or *Jack and the Beanstalk*! Yet to those who might doubt the authenticity of Christ's birth or even His historical existence, Matthew's family tree reveals Jesus to be the Jesus of history – we do not put family trees in fairy tales! As a result of the fact of Jesus' birth, we have to respond very differently to the Jesus of history than to some sort of fictional character. Matthew's Gospel tells us clearly from the outset, this is historical fact, this is truth, this is Jesus!

As we celebrate the birth of Jesus this year, two thousand and twenty two years after the first nativity, we celebrate that God Himself has broken into this world, in the flesh. Each of us are called to herald this, to announce the greatest day in history – the fact of God with us.

SCRIPTURE TO CONSIDER: Ps. 119:159–160; Luke 1:1–4; Heb. 13:7–8; Rev. 22:12–21

AN ACTION TO TAKE: What difference does it make to you knowing the reality of Jesus' existence?

A PRAYER TO MAKE: 'Lord, thank You that You broke into history, that You live today, that You call us to respond to Your call on our lives. Amen.'

Matthew 3:1–12

'In those days John the Baptist came, preaching in the wilderness of Judea and saying, "Repent, for the kingdom of heaven has come near."' (vv1–2)

The third chapter of Matthew's Gospel starts by telling us about the role of John the Baptist, a preacher calling everyone to 'repent for the kingdom of heaven has come near' (v2). Although many of the people John was preaching to were religious people, they had not seen the significance of Jesus, nor the significance of turning around from their current ways, to follow Him (vv7–10). John's message was clear, taken from the Old Testament book of Isaiah (Isa. 40:3), the people were to, 'make straight paths for [Jesus]' (v3b). The problem is that religion can often get in the way of truly seeing who Jesus is.

Perhaps at this time of year, we traditionally go to church, or perhaps we are regular churchgoers. Whilst it is important to gather with God's people, if it is a means in itself, such religious activity can take our focus away from the One we are called to follow – King Jesus. Or perhaps there are other distractions in our lives that take our time and attention, and before we know it, another year has passed, another carol service has been attended. Our call today is the same as it was for John the Baptist's listeners, to 'make straight paths' for Jesus, to be intentional in our following, to seek His will and ways for our lives each day.

Perhaps 2023 is the year that we 'make straight paths' that we might be used for His glory and Kingdom purposes.

SCRIPTURE TO CONSIDER: Josh. 1:1–9; Prov. 4:20–27; Phil. 3:7–14; Heb. 12:1–2

AN ACTION TO TAKE: What things might be distracting us from following Jesus wholeheartedly?

A PRAYER TO MAKE: 'Lord Jesus, help me to heed the call to follow You and to identify those things that take me away from following You each day. Amen.'

A Message of Hope

Isaiah 61:1–11
'The LORD has anointed me to proclaim good news to the poor. He has sent me to bind up the broken-hearted, to proclaim freedom for the captives and release from darkness for the prisoners, to proclaim the year of the LORD's favour and the day of vengeance of our God, to comfort all who mourn...' (vv1–2)

As we approach the Christmas celebrations, we also approach the end of another year. For some, this may mark a welcome conclusion to a challenging time, for others, it may have been a year of joy. In Isaiah chapter 61, God's people were in a dark place, with little 'cheer' – facing the consequences of their rebellion against God's Word and ways. Yet in the midst of challenge and dismay, Isaiah brings the people a message of hope. In spite of this dark season, the Lord, through His prophet, pointed the people forwards to a time when His kingdom would be visible and tangible, a time when the broken-hearted would be bound up, captives would be released, a year of the Lord's favour (vv1–2). A time when mourning would be replaced by joy, and despair replaced with praise (v3). Indeed, in Luke chapter 4, verses 18 and 19, Jesus quotes these very verses at the outset of His ministry, to signify the inauguration of God's kingdom rule.

Whatever our mood this Christmas, not only can we celebrate the amazing fact of 'God with us', but also the fact of God's visible kingdom, breaking into our world, becoming visible, touchable, realised in the ministry of Jesus. Furthermore, as God's people today, we too are called to participate in this kingdom project, which one day will be fully consummated at the return of Christ (Rev. 11:15). We too can bring a message of hope to those around us.

SCRIPTURE TO CONSIDER: Isa. 42:1–4; Jer. 29:10–14; Luke 4:14–21; 2 Cor. 5:16–20

AN ACTION TO TAKE: How might we bring a message of hope into the places the Lord has placed us?

A PRAYER TO MAKE: 'Lord Jesus, thank You that Christmas speaks to us of hope, a new birth, a new start, a new kingdom. Amen.'

2 Corinthians 5:16–20

'We are therefore Christ's ambassadors, as though God were making his appeal through us. We implore you on Christ's behalf: be reconciled to God.' (v20)

An ambassador has an important role, they literally represent a country or kingdom, whilst located within another country or kingdom! The embassies of various countries are 'little expressions' of the country to which they belong. It is the same for God's people today. As citizens of God's kingdom (Phil. 3:20), although we are located here on earth, we are expressions of God's kingdom.

The apostle Paul depicts this in his second letter to the Corinthians, describing them as 'Christ's ambassadors' (v20). Our role as His ambassadors is to represent Christ and His kingdom to a broken world, with the aim that people will be reconciled to Him as they hear His message of reconciliation (vv18–19). Christmas is the perfect time to announce this message, that reconciliation with the God who made and loved us is possible through Christ – that God Himself has provided a way, fully realised in the life, death, resurrection and ultimate return of Christ. What a great privilege it is to be considered His ambassadors! Wherever He has placed us, may we represent Him well.

> I am an ambassador for Christ, I represent my King
> I am an ambassador for Christ, His truth is what I bring
> I'll do my best to tell the world, What a wonderful King He is.
> In words and actions I will show, My neighbours I am His. *

SCRIPTURE TO CONSIDER: Isa. 52:1–12; Dan. 7:13–14; Rom. 5:1–11; Col. 1:15–23

AN ACTION TO TAKE: Think about the responsibilities of an ambassador to represent their country well – how might this translate to us as we represent Christ and His kingdom?

A PRAYER TO MAKE: 'Lord Jesus, thank You that You call us to be Your ambassadors, to participate in the reconciliation of men, women, children and young people to Yourself. Amen.'

* Garden Rose Music, 1995

Isaiah 52:7–10

'How beautiful on the mountains are the feet of those who bring good news, who proclaim peace, who bring good tidings, who proclaim salvation, who say to Zion, "Your God reigns!"' (v7)

In the midst of darkness and despair, Isaiah chapter 52 proclaimed hope for the people of God. The message of verses 7 through to 10 is a great message for us to share this Christmas too. Isaiah announces it as 'good news' of 'peace' and 'salvation' (v7), something to shout about (v8)! A message that causes God's people to sing, a message that brings comfort and speaks of redemption (v9) – something for all nations (v10).

This was welcome news of hope from Isaiah to a people thirsty for good news in the midst of their challenges and struggles. The current times we find ourselves in are also dark times for many people. People caught in conflict and war, or perhaps those with relational or other life challenges. The Christmas message is also a message of good news. A message that declares the peace and salvation available in Christ, a message to shout and sing about. In the midst of life's challenges, Christmas speaks of comfort and redemption, available for all people.

As we go about our everyday business this Christmas season, we too can spread this good news message – perhaps in the way we treat people, or how we share the good news of the gospel as the Lord opens opportunity to do so. Wherever we place our feet this Christmas, they can be beautiful feet as we share the message of hope and reconciliation.

SCRIPTURE TO CONSIDER: Ps. 98:1–9; Isa. 44:23; Nahum 1:15; Mark 1:1–3

AN ACTION TO TAKE: How beautiful are our 'feet'? How might we use each day to bring a message of hope?

A PRAYER TO MAKE: 'Lord Jesus, thank You that in the midst of bad news, You bring good news – something to sing and shout about. Amen.'

Mark 1:1–8
**'The beginning of the good news about Jesus
the Messiah, the Son of God...' (v1)**

At the beginning of Mark's Gospel, he gets right to the point, no second guessing what his message is about, 'The beginning of the good news about Jesus' (v1). Mark leaves us with no illusions as to what he is writing about. In the rest of the Gospel, as the other Gospel writers do, Mark tells us what Jesus *said* and what Jesus *did*, so we can know *who He is*.

Christmas can be a busy time, with lots of things to plan, perhaps presents to wrap and people to visit. In the busyness of the celebrations, it can be easy for the focus on Christ and God's redemptive activity, to be pushed to the side, or worse, not to feature at all. Like Mark, we need to be clear, leaving people with no illusions as to what we are celebrating and why – making the good news of Jesus 'up front and central'. Additionally, we need to communicate that the birth of Christ is just the 'beginning'; that the good news goes on to embrace his life, death, resurrection and return. The challenge this Christmas, for all of us who profess to own the name of Jesus, is to keep Christ in the centre in all that we do. The song says:

Jesus, be the centre
Be my source, be my light, Jesus.
Jesus, be the centre
Be my hope, be my song, Jesus.*

SCRIPTURE TO CONSIDER: Ps. 121:1–8; John 15:1–5; Heb. 3:1; 1 John 1:7

AN ACTION TO TAKE: How might we keep Jesus central this Christmas?

A PRAYER TO MAKE: 'Lord Jesus, thank You that You are the reason for the season. Help me to keep You central as I celebrate. Amen.'

*Michael Frye, 1999.

Cause for Praise

Luke 2:22–32

'When the parents brought in the child Jesus to do for him what the custom of the Law required, Simeon took him in his arms and praised God, saying: "Sovereign Lord, as you have promised, you may now dismiss your servant in peace. For my eyes have seen your salvation..."' (vv27–30)

L uke chapter 2 tells us that when the time had come, Joseph and Mary, in keeping with the Law of Moses, took Jesus to the temple in Jerusalem to be consecrated (vv22–23). A man called Simeon had been looking and waiting patiently for this moment, the fulfilment of God's promises to Israel (v25). As Simeon was holding Jesus in his arms, he could contain himself no longer – he burst into praise (v28).

It can be easy for us to lose hope and patience with our circumstances, sensing God has forgotten us or is not interested in our lives or situation. Yet whatever challenges we might be facing, Christmas gives us cause to burst into praise. As we consider the fulfilment of God's Old Testament promises, realised in Christ, like Simeon, we can give witness to the sovereign work of God (v29), declaring the peace of God in Christ who brings salvation and light to all who might look to Him.

This hope causes us to look beyond our *now* and to see the bigger picture of God's purposes, not only as we celebrate our own salvation made possible in Christ – but as we look to the final consummation of God's Kingdom rule.

SCRIPTURE TO CONSIDER: 1 Chr. 16:31–36; Ps. 7:1–17 & 100:1–5; Phil. 4:4–9

AN ACTION TO TAKE: Think of all that Christ means to us. Allow His Spirit to motivate us to praise and thanksgiving.

A PRAYER TO MAKE: 'Thank You, Lord, that whatever circumstances I am facing, I can praise You for the promises and hope I have in Jesus. Amen.'

Luke 2:33–40

'When Joseph and Mary had done everything required by the Law of the Lord, they returned to Galilee to their own town of Nazareth. And the child grew and became strong; he was filled with wisdom, and the grace of God was on him.' (vv39–40)

What a privilege and incredible responsibility it must have been to be Joseph and Mary, the earthly parents of Jesus, entrusted with the care of the long-promised Christ child. In verses 39 and 40 of Luke chapter 2, it tells us that following the consecration ceremony in Jerusalem, Joseph and Mary took Jesus home – they literally lived every day with Jesus! It was within this home that Jesus 'grew and became strong... [and] was filled with wisdom, [with] the grace of God on Him' (v40).

Through *Every Day with Jesus*, we want to encourage you to look to Christ each day, to know His presence and comfort as you navigate existing and new challenges. This is both a great privilege and a responsibility for each of us as we seek to grow in Him and learn how to walk and talk to Him each day. The words of the song capture this desire well when they say:

I want to walk with Jesus Christ,
all the days I live of this life on earth;
to give to him complete control
of body and of soul.*

SCRIPTURE TO CONSIDER: Deut. 6:1–9; Job 1:4–5; Dan. 6:10; Acts 17:10–11

AN ACTION TO TAKE: Waverley Abbey has a number of resources that can help you live every day with Jesus – why not visit our resources site today? You can find it at: www.waverleyabbeyresources.org

A PRAYER TO MAKE: 'Lord, help me to live every day with and for You. Amen.'
*Celebration Services (Yeldhall) Ltd, 1974.

Matthew 22:1–14
'Jesus spoke to them again in parables, saying: "The kingdom of heaven is like a king who prepared a wedding banquet for his son. He sent his servants to those who had been invited to the banquet to tell them to come, but they refused to come."' (vv1–3)

O ne of the things we associate with the Christmas celebrations is eating and drinking – a time, if we are so blessed, to celebrate with those we love. For others, it might be that we cannot be with those we love and care for, perhaps because of work commitments, geographical distance, or loss. If we are invited to dinner, we of course must accept the invitation in order for the hosts to expect and prepare for us, otherwise we will miss out. The kingdom of God is no different. Jesus spent a great deal of His ministry, teaching and preaching about the kingdom of God (Mark 1:14–15). In one of those times, recorded in both Matthew's and Luke's Gospel, Jesus told a parable about a king's wedding banquet. In this parable the banquet is prepared (v2), the king's servants are sent out to invite the guests (v3a). Their initial invitation is rejected (v3b), so a further and more urgent appeal is made (v4), only for this too to be rejected (v5). Later on in the parable, Jesus spells out the consequences for those rejecting the invite, including those who think they can gate crash the banquet on their own terms (v11–14).

Christmas is a time of invitation for all of us, to come to Christ, to worship Him, get to know Him and walk with Him each day. The invite comes out to us, by God's grace, year after year. Yet the Scriptures reveal that this will not always be, and that one day the invites will stop – it will be too late (Matt. 25:31–46).

SCRIPTURE TO CONSIDER: 2 Sam. 9:1–13; Matt. 25:31–46; John 2:1–12; Rev. 19:1–10

AN ACTION TO TAKE: Think about how you might share Christ's invitation to the ultimate banquet.

A PRAYER TO MAKE: 'Lord, thank You that You have called me to Your banqueting table. Amen.'

John 20:30–31
'But these are written that you may believe that Jesus is the Messiah, the Son of God, and that by believing you may have life in his name.' (v31)

People like stories. There is something about a story that we can immerse ourselves in, imagine ourselves in, relate to. Have you ever thought why we tell the Christmas story? Like the rest of the Bible, the Christmas story was written for a purpose. Towards the end of John's Gospel, John tells us that purpose, why he was inspired by God to write: 'that [we] may believe that Jesus is the Messiah, the Son of God, and that by believing [we] may have life in His name' (v31).

The Christmas story is not just a nice, memorable story, with wise men, shepherds, angels and of course the baby Jesus, but rather it was written for a purpose – to show us God's love and redemptive purpose for His created order, fulfilled in Christ as He grew to be the obedient servant (Phil. 2:6–8), taking the punishment that was ours on the cross, conquering sin and death (1 Cor. 15:55). As we grasp hold of this, and by faith put our trust in all that Christ has achieved for us, we too can have life, life in His name. The hymn says:

Tell me the story slowly, that I may take it in –
That wonderful redemption, God's remedy for sin;
Tell me the story often, for I forget so soon,
The 'early dew' of morning, has passed away at noon.*

SCRIPTURE TO CONSIDER: Ps. 107:1–3; Rom. 10:14–15; 1 Cor. 15:35–58; Phil. 2:6–8

AN ACTION TO TAKE: How would you share the Christmas story? Re-read it in Scripture, with a view to re-telling it to someone else.

A PRAYER TO MAKE: 'Lord, help me to tell Your story often, that others may also have life in Your name. Amen.'

*Katherine Hankey, 1866.

Gathered for a Purpose

Nehemiah 8:1–18
'All the people came together as one in the square before the Water Gate. They told Ezra the teacher of the Law to bring out the Book of the Law of Moses, which the LORD had commanded for Israel.' (v1)

Many people like to attend church services at Christmas time – these are often special times of gathering, with familiar carols and Bible readings. In the time of Nehemiah, after re-building the walls of Jerusalem was seen as an ideal time for the people to meet for worship – to give thanks to God who had brought them thus far. In chapter 8 of Nehemiah, we are given an insight into the elements of that gathering. It was a mixed assembly of people (v2), and as God's Word was read, the people listened attentively (v3). It was a time of worship (v6), where God's Word was also clearly explained (v8). The whole service was deeply moving, with expressions of weeping (v9), yet also joy (v10). Once the people understood the truth of God's Word, their joy was complete, and they celebrated with feasting (v12).

It can be easy to become over familiar with the Christmas celebrations – perhaps speaking of the 'usual' family, carol or Christingle service. Yet as we gather this Christmas, whatever form this may take, may we too seek to gain a true understanding of why we are gathered. May the truths of God's Word move us to such an extent that our Christmas celebrations take on a new meaning and purpose – making this year's Christmas celebrations truly life-changing and memorable, reminding ourselves of the deep meaning of this wonderful season.

SCRIPTURE TO CONSIDER: 2 Kgs 22:1–11; Neh. 1:1–11; Ps. 30:1–12; Luke 7:36–50

AN ACTION TO TAKE: This Christmas, ask God to give you an even deeper insight into His purposes and love for you.

A PRAYER TO MAKE: 'Lord, thank You for the many services and gatherings taking place this Christmas. May we truly grasp the depth and wonder of this season. Amen.'

Romans 8:31–39

'For I am convinced that neither death nor life, neither angels nor demons, neither the present nor the future, nor any powers, neither height nor depth, nor anything else in all creation, will be able to separate us from the love of God that is in Christ Jesus our Lord.' (vv38–39)

For many people, Christmas can be a sad time as they remember loved ones who are no longer with them. Perhaps others are separated by geography, or perhaps through work – those in the armed forces, for example. The constant images of family meals and celebrations can serve to amplify any feelings of loss or loneliness.

Practically, it is good for God's people to think about how we might reach out to someone feeling such loss at this time of year.

Yet, whatever loss or separation we may be feeling this Christmas, in the eighth chapter of Paul's letter to the Romans, he speaks about something that we cannot be separated from – the love of God (v39). Whatever our circumstances or situation – whether we are hospitalised, serving in the forces away from home, or grieving the loss of loved ones – God's love reaches us. And what is more, no powers or circumstances can separate us from this amazing love. Christmas reminds us of this as it tells us how God's love 'came down', dwelt amongst us (John 1:14). Whatever way we celebrate Christmas, whether it is with our wider group of family or friends, or in the quietness of our own home – reach out to God, receive His inseparable love.

SCRIPTURE TO CONSIDER: Deut. 7:9; Ps. 36:5–9; John 3:16–18; 2 Cor. 13:14

AN ACTION TO TAKE: Meditate on God's inseparable love for you.

A PRAYER TO MAKE: 'Lord, thank You that I can never be separated from Your love for me – Amen.'

A Time to Say Thank You

Philippians 1:1–11
'I thank my God every time I remember you.' (v3)

Christmas is often a time to say, 'thank you'. Perhaps we have received a gift from someone, or an act of kindness – or perhaps someone has tirelessly helped us throughout the year, and so we want to show our appreciation. The apostle Paul wanted to show his appreciation to the Philippian church that had encouraged and supported him. Writing from prison, Paul wrote the church an encouraging letter to thank them for their ongoing support and prayers. Although Paul was imprisoned and so could not be with them personally, he took the opportunity to write to them. In his letter, Paul pronounces upon them God's grace and peace (v2), thanks God for them (v3), and assures them of his constant prayers for them (v4). Paul goes on to remind them of their times together serving Jesus (v5) and encourages them by reminding them it is God who will see them through until the end (v6).

Perhaps we too could use this season to say 'thank you' – to call or write to someone to encourage them – to pray God's grace and peace into their lives, thanking God for them, assuring them of our prayers, reminding them of God's strength. Written words can be especially powerful as they can be re-read, allowing the recipient to dwell on them, and to be encouraged by them each time they are read.

SCRIPTURE TO CONSIDER: Ps. 136:1–26; Rom. 1:8–10; 1 Cor. 1:4–9; 2 Tim. 1:3–5

AN ACTION TO TAKE: Think of someone you could write to and encourage.

A PRAYER TO MAKE: 'Lord, thank You for the people You have placed in my life. Help me to encourage them in return. Amen.'

Colossians 1:15–20
'The Son is the image of the invisible God, the firstborn over all creation. For in him all things were created: things in heaven and on earth, visible and invisible, whether thrones or powers or rulers or authorities; all things have been created through him and for him.' (vv15–16)

As we celebrate Christmas, it can be easy to simply see Jesus as 'baby Jesus', a helpless babe. Yet in Paul's letter to the Colossian church, he gives us an awe-inspiring picture of just who Jesus is. Paul describes Jesus as the very image and reality of God Himself (v15), the One over all creation (v15). Writing to a church who knew God was the great Creator, Paul describes the divine Jesus as 'over all creation' (v15), with all things subject to Him (v16). Indeed, Paul goes on to describe Jesus as the very centre of the universe, the One who holds all things together (v17), One who also leads His Church in resurrection power (v18). Not to leave them in any doubt as to Jesus' identity, Paul reminds them again of His divine nature, with God's fullness 'pleased... to dwell in Him'. Ultimately, Jesus is the One who has made peace with God possible – all through His blood shed on the cross.

Next time we gaze at a nativity scene, if we are tempted to view Jesus simply as a helpless baby, let us be reminded that He is the supreme Son, in whom the fullness of God was pleased to dwell, and who has made peace with God a reality for all of those who would acknowledge the cross and bow the knee to Him as Lord.

SCRIPTURE TO CONSIDER: Dan. 7:13–14; Matt. 8:23–27; Mark 8:27–30; John 14:5–14

AN ACTION TO TAKE: Considering our scripture today, think about who Jesus really is. Write down your thoughts and give thanks.

A PRAYER TO MAKE: 'Lord Jesus, thank You that You are Lord of all. Help me to see beyond the manger and to help others to do the same. Amen.'

Much to be Thankful for

Ephesians 1:1–14

'Praise be to the God and Father of our Lord Jesus Christ, who has blessed us in the heavenly realms with every spiritual blessing in Christ.' (v3)

Many people on Christmas Eve, especially the young, are excited by thinking about what they might receive under the Christmas tree the next day. Maybe it will be that much longed for toy or gadget. As we get older, even the smallest gift matters – it is an indication that someone cares for us.

Whatever we may or may not receive this Christmas, as God's people we have so much to be thankful for already. The apostle Paul captures this in his letter to the Ephesians when, in chapter 1, he reminds the church of the many benefits they have as followers of Christ. Firstly, the blessings they have are not material, but spiritual (v3). They have been chosen, set aside to be His holy people (v4). They have been adopted into His family – a supreme act of love, which gives God great pleasure (v5). They are recipients of His grace, His undeserved favour, through Christ (v6). In addition to all of that, they have been saved, redeemed (v7), His love lavished upon them (v8), and they have been let in on His eternal plans for the universe (vv9–10). As God's people today, all of these blessings are ours too. Nothing we can receive in material terms can ever top this! We have so much for which to be thankful!

SCRIPTURE TO CONSIDER: Jer. 31:3; Luke 15:11–32; Rom. 1:7; 2 Cor 8:7

AN ACTION TO TAKE: Ponder the spiritual blessings Paul talks about in Ephesians 1. Think about how you might share what God has done for you with someone else.

A PRAYER TO MAKE: 'Lord God, thank You for the many spiritual blessings You have lavished upon me. Amen.'

Beyond the Baby

Luke 2:8–12

'But the angel said to them, "Do not be afraid. I bring you good news that will cause great joy for all the people. Today in the town of David a Saviour has been born to you; he is the Messiah, the Lord."' (vv10–11)

Growing up physically is a natural and expected reality for the majority of people. Growing up emotionally into mature adults is also expected but can vary greatly from individual to individual. This is a normal and accepted part of life. Yet when it comes to Christmas, many people celebrate the season, and perhaps use the occasion to attend a church service, yet somehow never allow Jesus to grow up, constantly singing about Jesus the baby.

In Luke chapter 2, when an angel of the Lord appeared to the shepherds (v9), the angel immediately encouraged the shepherds to think beyond the baby by announcing, 'Today in the town of David a Saviour has been born to you, He is the Messiah, the Lord' (v11). The angel could have simply announced the birth of a baby, yet he was able to look beyond the manger and speak of One who was the Saviour, the Messiah, the Lord. These loaded titles spoke of Jesus as One who would ultimately save the people from their sins, reconciling them to God the Father; One who would bring in a new kingdom rule as Messiah; and One who as Lord of all, would ultimately reign over all. As we celebrate the One born this happy morning, may we too be able to look beyond the baby.

SCRIPTURE TO CONSIDER: Isa. 9:6; Matt. 6:13–20; Col. 1:15–20; Rev. 1:9–20

AN ACTION TO TAKE: Think beyond Jesus the baby – what does Jesus as Saviour, Messiah and Lord mean to you?

A PRAYER TO MAKE: 'O Lord, help us to see beyond the manger and allow You to grow up in our hearts, that we might truly see who You are. Amen.'

1 Thessalonians 1:4–10

'The Lord's message rang out from you not only in Macedonia and Achaia – your faith in God has become known everywhere. Therefore we do not need to say anything about it…' (v8)

In the UK, it is quite common to hear the sound of church bells ringing. These bells are often used to call local people to worship, or perhaps to hail special events. Celebrating the birth of Jesus and announcing services to celebrate this are such occasions.

Yet long after the sound of the bells has died down, there is another type of 'ringing out' that the apostle Paul talks about to the Thessalonian church – the faith of God's people ringing out as they live each day for Christ. In fact, a life faithfully lived for Jesus is so powerful that, in itself and without words it 'speaks' of the love and grace of God (v8). Such was the faith of the Thessalonian believers that their faith had 'become known everywhere' (v8).

Long after the Christmas celebrations have died down, as we go about our daily business – be that in our communities, workplaces or homes – what 'sound' will our faith make? Will our example of Christ-following 'ring out' for everyone to hear? Like the Thessalonians, may our faith model to a watching and listening world what it means to follow Christ.

SCRIPTURE TO CONSIDER: Gen. 39:21–23; 1 Cor. 11:1; Phil. 3:17; 1 Pet. 2:12

AN ACTION TO TAKE: Think about the 'sound' our faith makes. What example 'rings out' from our daily lives?

A PRAYER TO MAKE: 'O Lord, thank You that You call us to model what it means to follow You. May our lives be a true call to those around us, to come worship and follow You also. Amen.'

Hebrews 11:1–40
'These were all commended for their faith, yet none of them received what had been promised, since God had planned something better for us so that only together with us would they be made perfect.' (vv39–40)

Hebrews 11 gives us a list of people considered to be heroes of faith in the Old Testament. People who heard God's call, and obediently stepped out to follow His purposes for their lives. People like Abel (v4), Enoch (v5), Noah (v7), Abraham (v8), Sarah (v11) amongst others. The Hebrews writer is careful to remind us that the list is not exhaustive (vv32–37) – many others also heeded God's call and 'by faith' chose to follow His plans rather than the short-term pleasures and pursuits of this world – they were looking for a 'better country' (vv13–16).

As we head toward a new year, it is common to make plans or have new hopes – yet this must always be done in the light of the fact that this is not our home – we too, are looking for a 'better city'.

As people who have trusted Christ, we too join this procession today, as fellow citizens with those who have gone before (Phil. 3:20). Our faith works in exactly the same way: God personally calls us, He gives us His covenant promise, we are called to respond – and as we do so, by His grace and empowering Spirit, we too are included as those justified by a common faith (Rom. 4:18–25), taking our place in His kingdom service.

SCRIPTURE TO CONSIDER: Gen. 6:11–22 & 15:1–6; Rom. 4:18–25 & 10:10

AN ACTION TO TAKE: Ponder: How are we demonstrating our heavenly citizenship?

A PRAYER TO MAKE: 'O Lord, thank You that You call me, by faith, to take my place in Your kingdom service. Thank You that the cross has made that possible. Amen.'

Focused on Him

Hebrews 12:1–3

'Therefore, since we are surrounded by such a great cloud of witnesses, let us throw off everything that hinders and the sin that so easily entangles. And let us run with perseverance the race marked out for us, fixing our eyes on Jesus, the pioneer and perfecter of faith.' (vv1–2a)

Having just given us an impressive list of Old Testament saints who all 'by faith' followed God's purposes for their lives, it would have been understandable if in the next section of his letter, the Hebrews writer exhorted us to 'be like them', to follow their example. Yet if we know anything about the people in the prestigious Hebrews 11 list, we know that they were human like us, with flaws and failings. It is not surprising, therefore, that the writer goes on to ensure the focus of his original readers, and ours today, is on Christ, exhorting us to, 'fix our eyes on Jesus, the pioneer and perfector of our faith' (v2a).

It is important that God's people encourage one another in their daily walk with Christ (Heb. 10:25). Also, we can strive to model what it means to follow Christ and be encouraged by the example of others (Heb. 13:7). Yet we need to remember that we are only human, as the Lord knows and reminds us in Psalm 103, verse 14. Like the saints of old, we can fail, let people down and behave out of character. So, like the original recipients of the letter to the Hebrews, we too need to ultimately focus on Christ as an example of endurance and strength (vv2b–3). As we focus on Him, we can have confidence that the pioneer and perfector of our faith will sustain us to the end.

SCRIPTURE TO CONSIDER: Ps. 103:1–22; Isa. 31:1; 1 Cor. 9:24–27; Phil. 3:1–14

AN ACTION TO TAKE: Where is our focus each day? Who do we look to for encouragement in our daily walk with Christ?

A PRAYER TO MAKE: 'O Lord, thank You for the people You have placed around me to encourage me in my daily walk with You, but help me ultimately to look to You as the great pioneer and perfector of my faith. Amen.'

THURSDAY 29 DECEMBER   Repeated Encouragement

Joshua 1:1–9

'Have I not commanded you? Be strong and courageous. Do not be afraid; do not be discouraged, for the LORD your God will be with you wherever you go.'' (v9)

There are some things that we need to hear time and time again for them to sink in. Perhaps this is due to distractions, inner fears or straightforward rebellion, a refusal to heed wise words. In Joshua chapter 1, we read of a pivotal moment in the history of God's people – Moses, the faithful servant of the Lord has just died (v1), and now it is Joshua who is called to lead the people into the promised land – to take on the mantle of leadership. This must have been an overwhelming situation for Joshua: grieving the death of his mentor Moses; the concerns, worries and responsibilities of the people before him. Joshua would need repeated encouragement. This comes in the form of God's words, where three times the Lord exhorts Joshua to be 'strong and courageous' (vv6,7 and 9).

We are also blessed by God's Word: it comes to us to encourage us, to teach us, to train us, to exhort us (2 Tim. 3:16). Yet sometimes, like Joshua, we need 'repeated encouragement' – to hear the same things over and over again for us to grasp what the Lord is saying to us, and to help us all as we move forward in service together. Perhaps we need to ask ourselves: How might I repeatedly encourage someone to live every day with and for Jesus?

SCRIPTURE TO CONSIDER: Judg. 20:22; Ps. 10:17; Acts 15:32; 1 Thess. 5:11

AN ACTION TO TAKE: Ponder God's repeated exhortation to be 'strong and courageous'. How might we pass on this encouragement?

A PRAYER TO MAKE: 'Thank You, Lord, for Your words of encouragement that challenge and uplift me. Amen.'

Joshua 1:10–18

'**Then they answered Joshua, "Whatever you have commanded us we will do, and wherever you send us we will go. Just as we fully obeyed Moses, so we will obey you. Only may the LORD your God be with you as he was with Moses."'** (vv16–17)

O nce Joshua had taken over the leadership mantle from Moses, and had received his instructions from the Lord, he faithfully passed these commandments on to the people (vv10–11). The people responded to Joshua with great enthusiasm, saying, 'Whatever you have commanded us we will do, and wherever you send us we will go' (v16). Although the rest of the book of Joshua reveals varying degrees of obedience and adherence from the people, what an encouragement it must have been to Joshua to hear this response.

As we end a year and head towards a new one, these words from Joshua 1 would be a fitting 'motto' for each of us, as we seek to serve the Lord wholeheartedly. Determining in our hearts to do 'whatever and wherever' for King Jesus, as His allegiant followers, is a high yet worthwhile goal. Whilst we know that each year brings setbacks and disappointments, there is a saying that 'if we aim for nothing, we usually hit it'! Perhaps, this coming year, with the Lord's help, as we focus on Him, we can be open to His leading 'whatever' that looks like and 'wherever' that may be.

SCRIPTURE TO CONSIDER: Ps. 31:3; Isa. 6:1–8; Jonah 1:1–17; Acts 9:10–19

AN ACTION TO TAKE: Are we brave enough to say to the Lord, 'whatever and wherever', Lord, use me?

A PRAYER TO MAKE: 'Thank You, Lord, that You call me to step out for You. Help me to fully trust You. Amen.'

Philippians 3:10–14
'But one thing I do: forgetting what is behind and straining towards what is ahead, I press on towards the goal to win the prize for which God has called me heavenwards in Christ Jesus.' (vv13b–14)

Pressing on and going all out for God is an admirable desire, yet it is important to be realistic about the challenges ahead and our own frailties. For our final message of the year, we want to encourage you to keep pressing on 'every day with Jesus'. To help here, our final encouragement comes from the apostle Paul, who knew what it was to struggle, suffer and strive for Christ (2 Cor. 11:16–33). In his letter to the Philippian church, Paul is realistic about his progress. Having expressed his desire to know Christ intimately, both in His power and suffering (v10), Paul is realistic enough to state, 'Not that I have already obtained all this or arrived at my goal' (v12a). Yet this did not deter him – in fact more the opposite. He goes on to say, '...but I press on to take hold of that for which Christ Jesus took hold of me' (v12b). Then, referring to whatever has gone on in the past, good or bad, he acknowledges that his focus needs to be on 'straining towards what is ahead... [pressing] on towards the goal to win the prize for which God [had] called [him] heavenwards in Christ Jesus' (vv13–14). As we enter a new year, whatever has gone on before, good or bad, we can thank God for the good things, the successes, His blessings – yet we can also learn from the challenging things. Perhaps some things we need to repent of, whereas other things were outside of our control. The important thing now for all of us is to 'press on in Christ Jesus', seeking to live every day for Him. We hope in the coming year, should the Lord tarry, that we will be able to encourage all of us to press on – to strive for that goal, that prize, as we seek to fulfil our calling in Christ.

SCRIPTURE TO CONSIDER: Gen. 15:1; 2 Cor. 5:9; 2 Tim. 4:8; 1 Peter 5:4

AN ACTION TO TAKE: Reflect on the past year, good and bad. Give it to the Lord – use it to motivate you for the coming year.

A PRAYER TO MAKE: 'Thank You, Lord, that You have sustained me throughout this year. May You strengthen me to "press on" towards my heavenly calling in Christ Jesus. Amen.'

Order form

Sign up to regularly receive your free printed copy of Every Day with Jesus (UK ONLY)

3 Easy Ways To Order

1. Visit our online store at **waverleyabbeyministries.org/edwj**
2. Send this form together with any payment to:
   CWR, Waverley Abbey House, Waverley Lane, Farnham, Surrey GU9 8EP
3. Phone in your credit card order: **01252 784700** (Mon–Fri, 9.30am – 4.30pm)

Your Details

Full Name: CWR ID No. (if known):

Home Address:

       Postcode:

Telephone No. (for queries):   Email:

Standard or Large Print (If left blank you will receive 1 copy of standard print.)

Standard ☐   Large Print ☐   How many copies of the printed notes would you like? _____

Regular donation

Please charge my account £ _____ monthly

CWR Instruction to your Bank or Building Society to pay by Direct Debit

Please fill in the form and send to: CWR, Waverley Abbey House, Waverley Lane, Farnham, Surrey GU9 8EP

DIRECT Debit

Name and full postal address of your Bank or Building Society

To: The Manager   Bank/Building Society

Address

Postcode

Name(s) of Account Holder(s)

Branch Sort Code

Bank/Building Society Account Number

Originator's Identification Number

| 4 | 2 | 0 | 4 | 8 | 7 |

Reference

| | | | | | | | | | | | | | | | | | |

Instruction to your Bank or Building Society

Please pay CWR Direct Debits from the account detailed in this Instruction subject to the safeguards assured by the Direct Debit Guarantee. I understand that this Instruction may remain with CWR and, if so, details will be passed electronically to my Bank/Building Society.

Signature(s)

Date

Banks and Building Societies may not accept Direct Debit Instructions for some types of account

Continued overleaf >>

<< See previous page for start of order form

One-off Donations

☐ I enclose a cheque made payable to CWR for the amount of: **£** _____

☐ Please charge my credit/debit card. **£** _____

Cardholder's Name (in BLOCK CAPITALS) _____

Card No. ⬚⬚⬚⬚ ⬚⬚⬚⬚ ⬚⬚⬚⬚ ⬚⬚⬚⬚ ⬚⬚⬚⬚

Expires End ⬚⬚ ⬚⬚   Security Code ⬚⬚⬚

Gift Aid (your home address required, complete above)

giftaid it   I am a UK taxpayer and want CWR to reclaim the tax on all my donations for the four years prior to this year **and on** all donations I make from the date of this Gift Aid declaration until further notice.*

Taxpayer's Full Name (in BLOCK CAPITALS) _____

Signature _____ **Date** _____

*I am a UK taxpayer and understand that if I pay less Income Tax and/or Capital Gains Tax than the amount of Gift Aid claimed on all my donations in that tax year it is my responsibility to pay any difference.

All CWR Bible reading notes are also available in single issue **digital** format.

Visit **waverleyabbeyministries.org/edwj** for further info.

For a subscription outside of the UK please visit waverleyabbeyministries.org/edw

How would you like to hear from us?

We would love to keep you up to date on all aspects of the CWR ministry, including; new publications, events and courses as well as how you can support us.

If you **DO** want to hear from us on email, please tick here [ ] If you **DO NOT** want us to contact you by post, please tick here [ ]

You can update your preferences at any time by contacting our customer services team on 01252 784 700.

You can view our privacy policy online at **waverleyabbeyministries.org**